Quit Your Job:

How to Live Out Your Dreams, Pursue The Work You Love & Achieve Financial Freedom

© Copyright 2019 by Oscar Monfort - All rights reserved.

This document is geared towards providing exact and reliable information in regard to the topic and issue covered. The publication is sold with the idea that the publisher is not required to render accounting, officially permitted, or otherwise, qualified services. If advice is necessary, legal or professional, a practiced individual in the profession should be ordered.

- From a Declaration of Principles which was accepted and approved equally by a Committee of the American Bar Association and a Committee of Publishers and Associations.

In no way is it legal to reproduce, duplicate, or transmit any part of this document in either electronic means or in printed format. Recording of this publication is strictly prohibited and any storage of this document is not allowed unless with written permission from the publisher. All rights reserved.

The information provided herein is stated to be truthful and consistent, in that any liability, in terms of inattention or otherwise, by any usage or abuse of any policies, processes, or directions contained within is the solitary and utter responsibility of the recipient reader. Under no circumstances will any legal responsibility or blame be held against the publisher for any reparation, damages, or monetary loss due to the information herein, either directly or indirectly.

Respective authors own all copyrights not held by the publisher.

The information herein is offered for informational purposes solely and is universal as so. The presentation of the information is without contract or any type of guarantee assurance.

The trademarks that are used are without any consent, and the publication of the trademark is without permission or backing by the trademark owner. All trademarks and brands within this book are for clarifying purposes only and are the owned by the owners themselves, not affiliated with this document.

Rituals Of The Rich & Famous

Success Tips, Strategies and Habits of The Rich & Famous

Get 4 new strategies every week on how to be more productive, confident, and happy.

Get Access Now

Contents

Introduction - False Realities

Signs You Need To Quit Your Job

The Aftermath of Quitting Your Job

Facing Your Fears, Crushing Your Goals & Eating Airplanes

Careers and Enterprise

More Satisfying Work

Build Your Dream Business

Lifestyle Design
    Travelling the World
        Make Money While Travelling the World
        Make Money Online

Financial Freedom

Staying Productivity Even if Your Lazy

Conclusion

Resources

Introduction - False Realities

Work, work, work …we spend most of our lives working. Go to school, get an education, get a job, get married, settle down, buy a house and plan for retirement. Then, and only then can you live out your golden years. From an early age most of us have been conditioned that a good education will result in a good job, a nice home, car and a stable life. Then if we work hard enough we will one day be able to retire and start to tick off all of those things from our bucket lists.

Sure one day you will probably have enough money to retire. That's as long as you work hard enough, spend a little and be a good employee. Just don't cause any trouble, listen to your boss, follow company policy and be an obedient employee. Keep doing that until your sixty five years or older and you too will be able to retire without ever having to worry about money again. But will you still have the health and mobility to enjoy life as you wish?

For the average person to retire will take about forty five years of work. And if you do get there, maybe after hoping for so long you just end up disappointed and find it to be anticlimactic. You end up too tired to go anywhere and spend your days binge watching netflix or complaining about the neighbours. This is a future that society is conditioned to manifesting. But the future is never certain and the so called dream we are sold doesn't apply to everyone. In reality, this doesn't have to be you.

With so much of our life time spent working it only makes sense to make sure you're getting the best experience possible out of your work. Right now if your not feeling happy with the job your in then it's time to take a new step. This book will help you to find out what that step is. Maybe it's time to quit your job and set up a business. Or maybe it could be time to go back to study, travel the world or even find a new job that is a much better fit for you. The essence of this book is about living your best life.

Today it is easier than ever to start and run a business from anywhere in the world. The internet and evolution of technology has made that possible. Contrary to what most people believe, there is in fact an abundance of jobs. You just need to approach things in a different way. There are many effective ways that you can easily find more fulfilling work or a businesses that fits with your lifestyle instead of your life fitting to the work. Then you won't have to miss your prime years and you can start living the life you want, right now. Give yourself the gift of being able to spend more time with your family, friends and travel as you wish.

Now this comes with a word of caution. Making moves to change your situation and live your best life is going to require you to start taking some risks. Getting from where you are now to where you want to be is going to require a leap of faith and maybe some false starts along the way. But go and ask any successful person. They will tell you the same thing. Anything worthwhile requires taking a leap of faith.

Taking risks is something people too often associate with negative attachment. But that's not what we are talking about here. It's not about risking your life or doing something without proper thought. No instead risk in this case means going after your dreams. It's about taking the risk of quitting a boring job for a better one or to create a business that fits with the lifestyle you want. That would be a calculated risk which results in positive outcomes. Taking a calculated risk in life will nine times out of ten enrich your life in many ways that you wouldn't even think of. Even if things don't necessarily work out the way you wanted there is always wisdom and lessons to be learned from any actions you take.

Calculated risks are always carefully thought out. Define the risks, define the rewards and weigh them up against each other. The reward versus the risk should be worthwhile and if it is you need to move forward swiftly. Once you become normalized to taking action quickly you will start to break free from the constraints of life and start to live your own way on your terms. New opportunities and better circumstances will come your way as a result. Now nothing is guaranteed if you do this. Sometimes you might be let down. But if you don't try, then you will never know.

Taking risks will open up a new world of challenge and opportunity that pushes growth and development in your life. New limits will be expanded in your mind and you will become more competent, strong and confident. We all have our own comfort zones and beliefs of what we think is possible. But let me tell you, you deserve more. Because you're reading this book it proves that you believe it too.

It's never too late to take control of your life. The biggest barriers you're going to face are your own fears. These fears are often much worse than what would you dread might happen. That's why there is a chapter dedicated to overcoming those fears. The first step is to identify where you want to go. You might have been stagnating for years, procrastinating on your decision. But you never know until you try and you will never quieten the questions in your mind until you take action. Trust your instincts and I know it sounds cliche, but listen to your heart.

Jordan Peterson says it all;

"You should be afraid of taking risks and doing something meaningful. But you should be more afraid of staying where you are if it makes you miserable but safe."

Maybe the risk of not doing anything is even bigger, after all you can accept your circumstances and avoid change. The problem is that most people simply accept the average way of thinking and have low expectations. Wake up and go to work, come home drained and watch the years slide by. They don't set goals or even question their circumstances. Instead they accept it all because thats all they see around them everyday and they believe that they have to keep working hard until retirement. They have been sold a false reality by the media and the people who want to keep us locked into this illusion. Most believe that the only way out of it is too "buy property" or "become a millionaire" or "get rich quick" or "get lucky" and various other bad anecdotal advice. Maybe in the past they get burned by some bad investment scheme and gave up.

The problem with the standard job/9-5 is that it limits how you spend your time and it limits your financial independence possibilities. There is a glass ceiling to it all. Now you might still think there is safety in having a job. But forget that. You could be laid off at any time. The company might be downsizing. Or your just not the right fit anymore. They can drop you within a month or less.

Wouldn't it be better to take a calculated risk in your favor? When you work for yourself or find a job where you're appreciated and your work is valued these kind of things are less likely to happen. In effect you will be in control of your income and lifestyle. The truth is that you decide on what it means to be free. That doesn't have to be a number in your bank account. Waking up to the ocean every morning or spending more time with your family doesn't require a million dollars in the bank.

Now this isn't some kind of conspiracy theory book against the current system. In fact there are some great benefits to modern society. Instead it's about expansion of your mind and seeing that there is a better life for you. Taking a different path, a path that aligns with what you want and not what others expect from you. I want you to live your best life because as a result this happening more people will start living this way and society will become better.

Think of it as a self directed life, living in alignment with your purpose, values, motivations, abilities and needs. Choose what you want to do and do it when you want. I know that might sound lofty and overly ambitious to you. But relax and open your mind. Give yourself a chance and let me show you how. Even if your married with kids or are older. With the rise of the internet there is much more potential for us to control our time and live on our own terms. Ultimately you can control your life and what happens day to day, year to year. More and more people are shifting towards independent lifestyles. Here are just some of the possibilities.

- Work just a few months out of the year
- Never work in an office - unless you want to
- Build multiple streams of income
- Travel the world
- Spend more time with family and friends
- Wake up when you want

Most people believe work has to be hard or boring. Then if your lucky if your work is enjoyable. Again it doesn't need to be that way. You can build a business on the side or find more fulfilling work. Long term if you want to live a fulfilled and happy life then evaluating your work life is crucial to that. Too much of your time is spent working, spend it on something that you enjoy. Now is the time, now more than ever before.

The other option you have is to stay where you are. Stay safe in that job you hate. It brings you a paycheck after all. But before you do that I want you to ask yourself one question. Do you think that things will be better in five to ten years if you stay in this job? If you answer no then it's time to evaluate where you really want to be. If your not sure then we can take a look later on at how to identify what is good for you and what is not. By all means, you don't necessarily have to quit your job. Maybe you just need to negotiate better terms. Or stay there and build a business on the side which you can later transition into.

This book will show you all of that and much more.

Signs You Need To Quit Your Job

Regardless of how much your paid at your current job it shouldn't mean settling for work you don't enjoy or that doesn't allow you to reach your full potential. Money is important but don't accept bad circumstances for more of it. Know your value because you also might not even be paid enough by your current job. If your constantly worried about money then you need to evaluate things. Maybe it's your spending habits or maybe it really is time for a pay rise. Consider the cost of your lifestyle. What do you really need? What do you do at work? How much should you be compensated for what you do?

If you have worked at a company for a while then you should be eligible for a pay rise. When negotiating make sure that your have a strong argument for why you should be paid more. If your employer doesn't agree to your new terms then it might be time to move on. Don't be fooled by the promise of a promotion because you could be waiting years for that. It's all just a case of them carrot dangling. Every year spent working needs to be evaluated.

Take the initiative, set a goal for when you want your promotion to happen by and set a figure in your mind. Then you can negotiate new terms with your current employer. Just be aware that they might decide to let you go anyway. If it's not about the money then be prepared to negotiate on the terms that you want to change. If it doesn't happen by then, move on. Ultimately you need to know your value and what your worth.

Living paycheck to paycheck can be frustrating existence. Time after time your always struggling to make ends meet.

Particularly if your in a full time job this shouldn't be the way to live for a long time. Now you might need to look at yourself first to check if your really being excessive with money in any area. That could be something as simple as your monthly rental costs. But if your living frugally whilst working full time then you need to question your salary. Because if you keep running out of money and relying on credit cards, loans or help from friends and family then you're digging a hole for yourself. Save the hassle and negotiate a better salary or find something that is better paid.

Taking action on the situation is really important and needs to be done as soon as possible. After all it's your life and you don't want to get stuck in a hole of debt. In the meantime you might need to work on a second job so that you can catch up on the bills. Additionally you should find ways to reduce your bills or even sell some of your things. Short term you will need to make sacrifices but in the long term you need to focus on higher pay. Set goals for what you want to earn and make sure those goals are realistic and specific.

Consider what is really bothering you about the job. When you get specific about whatever it is that you don't like then it will help you decide on what you do like. You might be proud to not call yourself a quitter. But in reality sometimes you have to do the best thing for yourself and that could actually be quitting. Times change, you grow and better situations will come along. If you wake up and dread going into work then it's time to have a rethink about your job. Don't lie to yourself here and downplay it as being a bad week. But also don't make decisions based on a bad day at work.

Are there specific tasks that you have to complete which bother you? Do you like the people you work with? Or are you just bored of the whole job? If you have been there for several years without any significant progression or satisfaction then it's time to move on. Sometimes it could just be that gut feeling that this line of work isn't right for you. The way you feel is pivotal to your success. If it doesn't feel right then it's not right. When this happens, pay attention and don't ignore it. We should always be on our way to becoming better versions of ourselves.

The problem is that most of us get stuck in our comfort zones at work. But in our comfort zone we are not growing. Eventually life will push us as it always does and we will inevitably go backwards. If your in a job that has just stagnated for months or years then you need to question whether it's time for a change. Don't be there just for the paycheck. Have a plan. If your not learning new things and are just doing the same old things then it's time for you to look elsewhere. Boredom is a key indicator of this. Without challenge we fall into boredom and doing things that we don't want to be doing or shouldn't be doing. We end up wasting time surfing online, playing games and generally wasting time. Eventually this starts to spill over into the rest of our life and dims it with you ending up like a zombie.

When you are no longer growing or no longer learning anything new then it's probably time for you to move on. If your an ambitious professional, which of course you are since you're reading this book. Well then you need to be challenged and escape comfort zones. Nothing can progress in those kinds of environments. Challenge stimulates growth.

Now on the flip side your job might be too challenging. Everyday this will wear you down and leave you feeling stressed out with no energy. If your in a situation like this then it's time to talk with your boss about responsibilities, compensation or leaving. Stress at work is all too common but it should not be happening every single day. If your boss expects too much of you then maybe you should find something where your appreciated more. Now in the worst case your health suffers and that is a serious sign that your job is taking way too much of you and you need to achieve a better work versus life balance. For many of us we struggle to switch between these two. If your work is draining all of your energy and you don't feel good about it then it will only get worse and start to negatively impact your personal life as well.

Generally if your in a toxic work environment then it's time to for your to move on. Signs of this include gossip and complaining. Now we all do this from time to time but if its a constant thing then it's not good for anyone at your work. The result of such toxicity is only going to create resentment and bad results. Maybe you don't like the way the company operates or the way people behave there. If so it's better that you find a place or line of work that you align with one hundred percent.

Finally leaving work could be something as small as the commute. If your wasting hours in traffic going to work there and back then consider your options. Do you really want to spend that much time commuting? Imagine all the hours wasted. Perhaps you should find something closer to home or something more location independent.

Key signs that you need to quit your job

- Not paid enough - know your value and what your worth.
- Frequently doing tasks which bother you
- Don't like the people you work with
- Frequently bored

- Always doing the same old things and not learning anything new
- The job is too challenging
- Too much stress
- Too much gossip
- Too many complaints
- Long commute
- Too much overtime
- Harassment

Stop being a victim

Health problems, stress and worry are just a few of the negatives that a bad job situation entails. We've all experienced this at least once in our lives. However there is a bright side to having a bad job…Am I being serious? Yes, please bare with me. First of all a bad job situation is incredibly motivating to get you to change the way things are. Behind your negative feelings is energy and this can be used to push you to make the right changes.

Anytime you catch yourself thinking about how much you hate the job reframe those thoughts into doing something proactive. Turn your attention to being solutions focused. Take many small actions to move away from your current situation. Actions such as applying for new jobs, making connections or researching a new business. Small actions snowball and soon enough you will be far away from the problem job. Hating your job could turn out to be the catalyst to a big positive change in your life. Stop making excuses and start making moves. List all the things you hate about your job and reframe them into steps your going to take and a situation that you prefer.

- Bad boss - become my own boss or work somewhere I am valued
- Long commute - find work closer to me or work that is location independent
- Low pay - negotiate new terms with my current employer or find a better offer
- Stress - find a job that suits my skills better or negotiate responsibilities with my current employer

Decide if you really need to quit your job or make negotiations to improve your current job. For a start you could still keep working at your job but make moves to go into business. In that case, have a talk with your bosses about reducing your hours. A colleague of mine recently did this and he is making big moves into running his own business. He was able to reduce his hours in exchange for a reduction in pay relative to the hours reduced whilst also retaining all the employee benefits. This allowed him the time to focus on building up his business whilst still having a stable paycheck.

Over the last five years the illusion of job security has become less and less likely. Gone are the days when you could work for one company for your whole career. Sometimes that can still happen but the truth is that most businesses are ultimately looking out for their own interests. The market is more fickle which means the employees are merely expendable. Financial gain is the driving factor and the bigger corporations will be even more focused on that. If business needs to be cut back then employees will suffer first. Don't let the illusion of job security stop you from going after your dreams. It's better to take calculated risks. After all companies go broke and management changes. They could cut you out at any moment and most contracts last for one year at the most. The world is moving more and more to independent working environments. You should at the very least have some kind of side hustle.

However if you enjoy being part of a big company then you better still take responsibility. Don't do it for just the money and security. Become indispensable and become a crucial part of the company. If you can become a key player then it will work out well for you. When those cutbacks happen you will be safe. Ultimately that could be a job for life, if you want.

Take full responsibility for your future security. Never be dependent on a company for your future livelihood. The responsibility ultimately ends with you. The less dependent on a company you are the more choice you have. This is great for when you come to negotiate new terms or are looking for new jobs. You will have much more freedom, time to make better decisions.

The dilemma of most employees is that they are depending on just one source of income. The best solution is to constantly update your skills and find new opportunities. It's about getting out of your comfort zone which can be a dangerous place. When it comes down to it, the drive behind a career must come from the individual. Whilst you have your job, even if you want to work for a company forever make that side hustle happen.

Make a plan and change your life for the best.

The Aftermath of Quitting Your Job

Before you quit your job and leave there are some important points to think through. One more time before you formally resign take some time to consider whether or not you really do want to quit. Remember not to make this kind of decision in the moment because of your emotions. If its a bad day face the next day fresh and review the whole job over a longer period of time. Make it a calculated decision. Create a list of all the things you hate about the job versus all the benefits. Weigh those up against each other and ask yourself if you are willing to work there longer or if you are ready to face a new challenge? Do you have something else lined up? What about negotiating better terms? Remember that once you have handed in your resignation your employer will look to fill your position quickly.

Quitting your job can be a necessary step to take at some point and if you feel it's time to move on then there are some things you need to be aware of before you do. First of all, make sure you leave on good terms. References are pretty useful if you plan to stay on the employment circuit. The way you leave a job will influence the kind of reference you receive. Even if you don't list your supervisor your future company will still likely come into contact with them. Reputation is everything in the business world.

Leaving on good terms also extends to your colleagues who might feel hurt or offended about you leaving. Again make sure you leave on good terms with them as well. Later they could become your allies and supporters. A simple explanation as to why you leaving should suffice. If you value them go for a drink or meal out to talk about you leaving or to celebrate the next step.

On a personal level quitting your job will affect your mood. The feeling of being a quitter or being called a quitter can impact your emotions. Feelings of disappointment and guilt may arise if you don't pay attention to your mind state. Realize that rather than being a quitter you made the decision to positively change your life.

The most noticeable effect of quitting a job will be the dip in finances. Unless you have another job or income ready to go then you are going to feel the pinch. There also will be a loss to the benefits associated with a job such as health insurance or accommodation. Make sure you're well prepared in advance. Finding a new job can take a long time so it's always a good idea to have something else lined up to transition into. Consider if you have enough savings to cover any periods of unemployment. Even better if you have a business that's bringing in money each month or a new job lined up. Having an emergency savings fund is also an excellent plan and we will discuss that later on.

Give Adequate Notice

When you're sure that you want to quit your job you need to handle your resignation as professionally as possible. In your employment contract there will be a condition for how much notice you should give, abide by it. In most cases two weeks to one month is the standard protocol. During your last few weeks it's really important to conduct yourself professionally and keep adding value until you go. Also you will need to enquire about collecting any unused vacation and any benefits along with how they will be handled moving forward. If you have any company property make sure you return it before leaving.

The formal way to resign is by resignation letter and to also let your employer know in person. But depending on circumstances quitting by phone or email may be more relevant. In your resignation letter its best practice to focus on the positives and the ways in which the company has benefited you. Offer an explanation as to why your leaving. For example explain that it's time to move on with a new challenge. Keep it positive and don't be negative. Let them know when your last day will be and be prepared for any exit interview which they may require. Finally before you leave, ask your boss for a reference. If they can prepare you with a written letter or agree to talk to your future employers then it's great to secure that in person before leaving the company. Again always leave on good terms. Here is an example of a resignation letter format:

[Your name]
[Your Address]
[Date Today]

[Recipient name]
[Title]
[Organisation]
[Address]

Dear [Manager Name],
Please accept this letter as notice of my resignation from the position of [Job title] at [Company name].

As per the terms of my contract, I will continue to work for the company for the next [notice period], completing my employment on [last day you plan to work].
It has been a rewarding experience being a part of the team and I am grateful for the opportunities you have given me during my time here. Please let me know if there are any

particular areas that you would like me to focus on during my notice period.

I hope that you can help me with a positive reference in the future.

Yours sincerely
[Your name]

Last days

When it comes to the day of you leaving make sure you have everything you need from your workspace and computer. Retrieve any important documents and anything of a personal nature. That could be things that you might use for future reference. If your employer asks you to stay longer then remember that you are not obliged to. However, it's up to you if you want to help your previous employer, with extra time or finding a replacement.

It can be a strange feeling at first to not have a job to go to but it is also going to feel incredibly liberating. In front of you will now be more choices than you ever had before. Take your time to get into a new routine. You don't need to jump right into something else. Allow yourself time to adjust and maybe even learn new skills and to adjust your priorities. Consider what it is you really want and avoid being impulsive or reactionary.

Rushing into the next job or business might have an adverse affect on your future. In the next chapter we will take a look at how to find out what it is you really want to do and how to make a solid plan to achieve it.

Face Your Fears, Crush Your Goals & Eat Airplanes

Acknowledging that it's time to quit your job can be a daunting thing. The reality is that most people are afraid of the uncertainty it brings. Because of that they will often remain in a so called "stable" but unhappy work environment. Years slip by them as they suffer in quiet desperation. But it doesn't need to be that way. If the thought of quitting your job terrifies you then I'm here to help you overcome it. The key is to know what you want, analyze your fears and face them.

Our biggest fears are usually the things that we most need to do. Truth is that they are what is blocking us from fulfilling our dreams. In our minds we often make them much worse than the reality. I want you to ask yourself. What are you neglecting to do because of fear? Is it talking to your boss about a raise? Or is it actually quitting your job?

Tim Ferris the best selling author and multi-millionaire entrepreneur attributes fear setting with producing his biggest business and personal success as well as avoiding huge mistakes. In fact for him it is so effective that he practices fear setting almost every month. Now this is a detailed process but it is well worth it. I have adjusted the Time Ferris process somewhat to fit more with the core concepts of this book. If you're reading this book because you want your situation to change then you need to take these steps. Seriously, just reading a book won't change you. Go get a pen and some paper. Turn off your phone and without further or do, let's go!

Step One: Goal Setting

Goals are the match that starts the fire for going from where you are now to where you want to be. Sparks create epic fires. You see most people never do this kind of soul searching. Which is the reason why they stay stuck in jobs they hate. Stuck in a life that doesn't fulfill or inspire them. By exploring and questioning yourself it will ultimately help you to find a career and a life you love. Having clear goals will make you much more likely to succeed at whatever it is you want to achieve. Whether you want to quit your job and find a new one or start a business you need to know exactly what it is that you want.

Start by taking a journey in your mind right back to your childhood. During our childhood years is when our passions first become clear to us. But later on life distracts and pushes us away from what we really want. Getting back in touch with those feelings is an important step to finding what you're really passionate about. What did you dream about being when you grew up? What distracted your mind during class?

Who did you want to be? Take note of what comes up from this exercise.

Next, take time to ponder and write answers to the following. If you could start over again tomorrow what would you do? If you took money out of the equation. What would you really be doing? Don't censor yourself, write what comes out first. Maybe that's travelling the world, playing music or racing cars. Think of your idols, personally, professionally and online. Whose career would you most want to be doing? Find out what it is and write the answers down. You should have a good amount of text by now.

Finally think about and write down all the things that you are good at. Are you good with people, technology or planning? Are you skilled at something particular? Are there any memorable work experiences which you enjoyed or excelled at? If you can't think of what your good at then ask friends or family members. Consider, why would someone hire you and what value do you bring to the table? Write these all down.

Now if you're really struggling to identify your passions then ask your friends and family. Ask them what your talents are. Ask them what you seem to be happiest doing. Ask them what they think is a best fit for you. The answers they give you might come as a surprise. But listen to them with an open mind.

Now remember passion is not the only factor because you might be passionate about something but lack the gifts to accomplish it. For example you might want to be a ballet dancer but lack the flexibility. Or you might be passionate about being a lawyer but haven't studied law. However don't let that put you off. The truth is to recognize the curiosity you have for something and find something that aligns with that and your gifts. For example, if you are passionate about football but don't have the natural abilities then you could focus on the theory or techniques. Or if you lack certain credentials then you can go back to study. We will take a look at some of the options in more detail later on.

Your career doesn't need to be solely focused on stacking cash. If thats your main goal then you won't gain much satisfaction. Because there is much more to it if you want to have longevity. Ultimately, money should not be the defining factor. You must find meaning, purpose and accomplishment. Without that you will struggle to see it through.

After completing these exercises in finding out your true passions and interests you should have a big list. Start narrowing down that list to your most favorite. You can categorize them with A, B, C. The most important being A and downwards. Those main things should make you feel excited when you think about them. Allow yourself some time, a few weeks or so to really let them sink in because you might change them over time.

The final aim is to get specific on what your goal is. From your list of jobs narrow it down and be as detailed as possible. If you have about five different roles it will be fine. Ideally you should have one because the more specific it is, the more likely it will happen. That's how our minds work, just like a missile aiming at the target. If you still have too many then use the following questions to narrow it down more.

How much do you want to earn? What field do you want to work in? Do you want to work from home? Do you want to be part of a team? Is location important to you? Are you looking to negotiate better terms with your current employer? Consider all the possible scenarios and dreams. Write them down. Brainstorm all the careers and come up with lists. Don't censor yourself here. Anything goes! Just write down whatever comes into your mind. When your prune that list remove anything that doesn't spark any joy in you. Also remove anything that is unlikely to produce any decent money. Also remove anything that seems unrealistic to you. When you have your final list. Put your favorite at the top.

Now you should have a rough idea of whatever that job or business is or even the subject you want to study. Next you want to make sure your goal is measurable. Defining it should be as simple as having criteria to know when you have achieved it. That could for example be an amount of money, registering a business, a subject to study or starting a new job. Write it out and get clear on it. What you measure will be done and when you neglect to measure your progress towards your goals then you will be lost in a world of frustration and confusion. Get specific and write it all down.

At this point you should have a goal that is both specific and measurable. But is it attainable? At the end of the day your goal should be something that is possible for you to achieve. Now it doesn't have to be super eas. In fact something a little hard to achieve is great because it will challenge you and make you grow. But simply put there are somethings that we don't have full control over. If for example you are signed in a contract for a year and you want out in six months then you might need to reconsider the time frame. In the same regard the goal should also be realistic. Aiming for one million dollars a year when you haven't yet reached one hundred thousand a year would be a good example. Or getting a job as a lawyer without studying is also unrealistic.

Consider your circumstances, strengths and weaknesses when you set goals. Shoot high but be realistic otherwise you might lose sight and get fed up in the pursuit. Having unrealistic expectations is one of the most disheartening things because often they're not going to come true and then your going to feel disillusioned and want to give up.

The final part to setting a goal is the timeline. Start from the big picture and take it step by step backwards. Think about where you want to be in five to ten years. Once you've got it down think about where you want to be at the end of this year. This is your goal for the year. Now work back and reverse engineer it back to the months. What are the things you need to achieve by the end of the month and by the end of next month? Next break it down it into the weeks. What do you need to achieve on a week by week time frame? Going further break it down day by day. What are the things you need to achieve each day? Furthermore start looking at the day in detail. What do you need to do each hour from waking up to going to sleep. Approach each hour and execute because that is how you make progress and get things done.

Eating Aeroplanes

There are people out there who have eaten entire aeroplanes. For real, but you're probably thinking how can someone eat an entire aeroplane? Well what they did was to break it down into chunks. In fact they ground it down daily and with every single meal they ate it bit by bit over two years. Now I'm sure most of you have no goal to eat a plane, but you have a big goals. The way you approach them is the same. You break the goal down into smaller pieces that you can deal with on a daily basis. Then over time something monumental can be achieved.

These days people are addicted to social media because of the instant gratification it brings. Upload a post and you get your likes and comments right away. People have become wired to this instant gratification hook. Then when they attempt something longer term they just can't. Most people make the classic mistake of thinking that if it can't be done in the space of a day or a month at most then they don't even bother trying. The reality is that most things that are actually worthwhile take a much longer period of time and effort. The secret to achieving the big goals is to chunk them down. Just like the man who ate a plane took and took two years to do it.

Take your goal and break it down into small pieces. When you eat a steak you do it one bite at a time. When mountaineers climb a mountain they don't just stare at the summit. Because that is how you get disheartened and worn out. Release your attachment to the goal and stops fixating on flashy lifestyles. Instead learn from the mountaineers. Instead of focusing on the summit they stare at their boots. They focus on making another step. A step that brings them closer to the summit. Because if they focused on the summit it would seem much too far and overwhelming. So stop fixating on the goal and waiting for it to happen. Instead focus on what you can do today and chunk it down into bite-sized pieces.

Start with a daily plan and schedule your actions. Google calendar is a great tool for scheduling actions because you can take advantage of the reminders. These will be the habits and daily actions that lead towards completing your goal. Every step should be bringing you closer to the goal. Define what the most important steps are and prioritize them. At first it will be challenging but as you start to automate those tasks you will become much more effective. In the process you will learn how to maximize and manage your time.

Keep the following in mind, achieving goals is a marathon. It is not not a sprint and things take time. Especially huge changes. You need to approach your goals like you're approaching a marathon. Just like the rabbit racing the tortoise. The rabbit started out fast whilst the tortoise started slowly. But he stayed consistent and won the race whilst the rabbit gassed out and gave up.

Step Two: Fear

Now here comes the reality check. Say that you have a goal. This should be your major goal. This could be something such as starting a business or taking a year out to travel or going back to study. Whatever it is, define the worst things that could happen if things didn't work out. Write down all the worst possible outcomes and don't censor yourself. Define the very worst scenarios that you fear the most. Envision them and consider the impact they would have on your life. Come up with at least five scenarios for your goal. For example.

My Goal is to: Travel the world

What is the worst that could happen?
- Run out of money
- Fall sick
- Gap on employment history
- Hate it
- Family disagree

My Goal is to: Start a business

What is the worst that could happen?
- Failure
- Run out of money
- No free time
- Lose credibility
- Legal issues

My Goal is to: Go back and study

What is the worst that could happen?
- Denied
- Family disagree
- Run out of money
- Fail the course or entry

Now with these fears in mind and now visible to you it's time to look at solutions to fixing these issues if they indeed did happen. Let's take a look at the two examples.

My Goal is to: Travel the world

What are the solutions to these problems if they happened?
- Run out of money - work in a basic job
- Fall sick - go back to stay with my family
- Gap in employment history - most employers would be interested in someone with a passion for life. If you can make good reasons and make it sound interesting then it's much more enticing for them to employ you.
- Hate it - go back to a basic job for a few months whilst searching for a new one.
- Family disagree - they will eventually warm to the idea.

My Goal is to: Start a business

What are the solutions to these problems if they happened?

- Failure - lessons learned
- Run out of money - money can be made back, work part time or basic level jobs for a short period
- No free time - become more productive and master your time
- Lose credibility - every situation can be framed in a different light
- Legal issues - start small and have an emergency savings fund.

My Goal is to: Go back and study

What are the solutions to these problems if they happened?
- Denied - try a different university. This one isn't meant for you.
- Family disagree - they will understand if you sit down and explain everything
- Run out of money - save in advance, work part time, get a student loan
- Fail the course or entry - try a different university. This one isn't meant for you.

What you will notice when you come up with solutions to your fears is that a lot of them are not really that bad. Not only that but they will for the most part they will be temporary. Sure you might have to eat rice and beans or work in 7/11 for a bit. But that experience will humble you and ultimately bring you back stronger. In life we can recover very quickly. Plus don't forget that if things usually work out for the better.

"I am an old man and have known a great many troubles, but most of them never happened." —Mark Twain

So with the worst cases in mind now you need to define what the more positive outcomes could be and how likely they are to happen. Have people achieved these goals before? Did they have more or less of a chance than you? Think about all the costs of not taking action. Not just in a business cost but as a personal cost. Nine years ago I left my home country with $600 in my bank and one backpack of clothes. I flew to a foreign land and was offered the job of my dreams. My life has never been the same since. Our time is limited on this earth and if you don't pursue the things you want then your life won't change for the better.

My Goal is to: Travel the world

What are the best things that could happen?
- Get to see the world
- Live location independent
- Meet new people who share my goals
- Increased opportunities
- Life experience

My Goal is to: Start a business

What are the best things that could happen?
- Get rich
- Become my own boss
- Take care of my family
- Create jobs for people
- Become happier

My Goal is to: Go back and study

What are the best things that could happen?
- More fulfilling work
- Smarter
- More effective
- New connections
- New meaning to life

I hope this exercise has helped you to either plan your escape or to identify new opportunities based on your current skill set. Take the time to do the exercise and be really clear on exactly what it is that your going to do next. Failure to get clear will make it more likely for you to end up back in a job which you don't enjoy. Never be running away from what you don't want. Instead be running towards what you do want.

Careers and Enterprise

Once you have settled on a passion it's time to actually start doing it! Regardless of your age, background or experience you deserve a shot. Seek out advice on how to turn this passion of yours into a living. There a number of ways to do this. The first step is to start researching. Take a look at people who are actually doing it and if you can, get in touch with them. Talk to career counselors about your plans. Bounce ideas off them. Leverage social media and the internet. Look at all the blogs, profiles and so on.

After doing this you should have some pretty solid strategies. It doesn't have to be the biggest. There are thousands of opportunities in every passion. A good friend of mine travels the world making videos and then upselling products. Another finds various part time jobs wherever he goes to fund his travels. At the start you will need some cash flow or savings to get you going. But as traction starts to gain you can cut down your working hours and then move into pursuing your passion full time. Ultimately the only way to pursue those passions is to take action and try it.

Jobs come and go. Offers come and go. Brian Acton who sold Whatsapp for 18 Billion US Dollars was initially rejected by

Twitter and Facebook when applying for a job. I'm sure he would confirm that the key is persistence and belief even in the face of adversity. Stop thinking about what happened and instead focus on the future.

Would you rather be, an employee or an employer? Or maybe you want to reinvent yourself and go back to study? The lives and responsibilities of each options are quite different and it's important to be self aware of who you are and what you want. When your an employee it simply means you work for other people. In return for making money for them you receive a regular salary plus any other incentives and bonuses. Of course this is great for you if you prefer fixed hours and a regular, stable income. Getting up the ladder in the company will offer you a better pay and benefits. Although there is always the risk of not getting promoted or worse, getting fired. At the end of the day you will always have a boss to report to and company policies to follow. Keep in mind that some companies can be great to work for whilst some can be dreadful.

As an employer it means that you work for yourself and in most cases you will employ other people. Financially this offers much more potential for growth. But it also means you need to make money. As the owner of the business the responsibility ends with you. Success requires hard work, especially at the start. In fact, you will probably need to have weeks or longer without any earnings. Then there is no guarantee that you will succeed. Risks that you cannot predict can happen. Anything from politics, economy or finances can affect you. However if you are successful the lifestyle of a business owner can be very rewarding.

Learn what it takes to start a business. This should include everything from the legal to the technical aspects and more. Make sure you are covered financially and prepare for the worst case scenarios. Later on we are going to look at all of this and more in detail. During the research you might well find that your not really that interested. In that case you haven't really lost anything and you can move onto something else.

If you start a business and it doesn't work out then don't despair. Try something new. Most entrepreneurs have a string of failed businesses behind them before they strike gold. So think through the advantages and disadvantages relevant to you being employed versus being an employer. At the start you could be just one business owner. Then as you become more comfortable and grow you can start to bring in other people as your employees. Many people taking this route start out working from home. This can be a welcome change from having to travel to an office everyday and deal with the routine of office life. Not only that but you will be your own boss. No more ridiculous demands or policies that you have to follow!

At the end of the day you have to decide whether to be an employer, an employee or go back to study. Consider your strengths, weaknesses and preferences. Do you have the essential attributes required to be an employer? Leadership, persistence and patience are just some of those attributes. Are you willing to take a risk? Or do you prefer the comfort and stability of a paycheck? At the end of the day you and only you are responsible for your income, regardless of who you work for. Approaching your work in a passive way will not be enough. You need to become indispensable to your employer. Go the extra mile. Someone who is indispensable will always do more than what they have been asked for. Take your work seriously. It should be something that captivates and motivates you. This will encourage you to go the extra mile. Be constantly learning new things, attending conferences and studying. Knowledge is power.

Consider whether or not you're the type of person that is productive in office environments or alone. If you prefer office environments then you can still be an employer. Coworking spaces are becoming more and more common. They offer great facilities and very productive environments. In some cases you might even be able to negotiate working from home with your current employer. So much office work these days can be done via the internet and it would be fine with most employers. Consider what it is you want and then make the changes or negotiations necessary.

Alternatively it is quite easy to find jobs working from home and then you could transition to your own business. There are plenty of jobs out there that you can work from home on. Writing, design and IT are just a few of many more. There are various advantages working on a home based business such as tax advantages which can be written off as home expenses. That could include part of your rent or mortgage and even repairs. Plus you save money on commuting and car repairs. If a company employs you then it can be a tax advantage to them for letting you work from home and also to save money from having to set up an office. It's a win, win situation. Some of the advantages are fairly obvious, such as having a flexible schedule, freedom, and chances to earn more. It might make a lot of sense to start working at home. Maybe your a new parent and need to be working from home. Working at home allows you to make your own schedule and work as it suits you.

Where are you now?

If you are currently employed but are interested in starting a business, then right away you can start making some shifts towards being an employer. Be honest with yourself and explore your opportunities. If you need to learn more than attend some seminars or take a course. Going back to school can be a daunting prospect. For most of us it might feel like a step backward or you might feel too old for it. But in fact none of that is really true and it's all about how you frame the idea in your mind. For example, sometimes PhD or MSc qualifications are required in order for you to advance or to earn a higher salary. Ultimately this help you move forward or branch off into a particular specialism within your field.

The workplace is changing all the time and it's important to understand education is and the pursuit of knowledge is crucial to long term success. Today, you can never afford to stop learning. Remaining relevant will require new skills and training. Figure out the kinds of qualifications and certificates in the industry. Some could be taken on short term courses. Others require more long term qualifications. Adding these to your resume will always give you an advantage. Many technical and educational fields require professional certifications such as MBAs and MFAs. An MBA (Masters of Business Administration) is often a requirement in the finance sector. Whilst an MFA (Masters of Fine Arts) allows writers to teach at accredited universities and colleges.

Maybe you're stuck in a career that no longer makes you excited or satisfied. This is your chance to start fresh and find new career opportunities. If your going into a new field of expertise then this will be a massive help for you. Not only will gain the right qualifications you will also have valuable expertise in that particular area. It could even be a way to gain more knowledge and qualifications in your area right now. This would help you to gain a higher position.

At the start it makes sense to keep your job so you can have some money coming in. that means you could start a business or go back to study whilst still having an income. Later you can reduce your hours and then leave when the time's right. Many employers may well offer study programs as part of a career progression package. Now if you have been working for a while your likely to have other commitments such as raising a family. This will obviously constrict your time and responsibilities.

Study options

Many courses nowadays can be taken online, by distance learning, part time learning, accelerated learning or as a work based study. These options are great and will allow you to not compromise your current lifestyle whilst getting a good education. Maybe you didn't finish a degree, you could go back and complete that or even go onto a higher level such as a masters. Shaquille O'Neal and Steven Spielberg are just two famous people that returned to complete studies.

One of the most important factors of deciding to go back to study is costs. Going back to study has some serious financial implications. How much funding you have available to you will depend on your circumstances. If you have children then you may be eligible for a parents learning allowance. Check online for your particular region of the world. Some universities and colleges may also offer bursaries on the subject area you are interested in. Get in touch with the admissions office and also check the university website or ask the local authority. Your situation and whats available to you will depend on your income and eligibility.

Being outside of the learning system for a while is likely to make you doubt your ability to fit into education. Friends and relatives might have a negative reaction to you going back to study. Especially those from a more traditional background. Most likely they will tell you that it is selfish and financially risky. However at the end of the day, you know the real reasons why and it's your decision which should be taken carefully. If you have a family talk it through with them and make a plan. Be determined to show them the difference it will make in your life.

Going back to study as a mature adult can be a challenge. Especially if you have family and financial commitments. Luckily, there are a number of ways to easily go back to study. The Open University offers adult learners the option of enrolling in flexible part-time study programmes and distance or open learning for undergraduate and postgraduate courses. Studying part time is usually the best option for mature students. Usually your can pay per module. Although this overall can take longer to complete. Many universities will also offer extra support to students who struggle. Extra curricular activities in the areas where you are weakest should be taken. Take all of this into account when choosing a course. If there is something your feel you will need extra help on then check if there is support for it. It could be something as simple as computers, spreadsheets and so on.

When researching courses be on the lookout for those with flexible options on offer. Look for courses with online studies, weekend, evening or summer intensive programs. Even if most undergraduate courses run on daily schedules, some are also likely to be more flexible. In fact, many universities offer a flexible and part time schedule. If you are dealing with extra commitments it's a good idea to be organised ahead of time. last-minute rushing will cause stress and bad scheduling. Free up some time by hiring help or planning in advance. This will all pay off when your able to study with free and ease. Make the most of any support services at the university, whether it be counselling or extra skills classes. Explain your circumstances to the lecturers and staff at the beginning of studying so that they are aware of your needs.

Remember that maturity and experiences will add a lot of value. Now more than ever, people of many ages are deciding to go back to study or education at an older age. According to 2012 statistics from the National Center for Education Statistics more than forty percent of the students in the United States were over twenty five years of age. Whilst UK-based Universities and Colleges Admissions Service (UCAS) found that students over the age of thirty accounted for over forty percent of students. Many universities and colleges now offer programmes specifically-tailored for adult learners.

As an adult student, you will be more eager and serious about learning. When your a teenager it's more about the lifestyle and the partying. Being an adult at university is a smart move and you will gain much more from it. Challenges can be approached with maturity and information deconstructed effectively. Fundamentally mature students are there to learn. Michelle a 32 year old went back to study after a career as a personal assistant. "Going back to education later on refreshed my life purpose and gave me a new motivation for a better career"

When you know what it is you want to study look for programs that produce practical skills. Get in contact with the lecturers and students if possible to have there feedback on your plan. This could be concluded from a visit there. In addition ask professionals working in that field how they got there. Ask if there was any specific king of training involved. You can find these people on linked in or at networking events for the industry. At the end of the day make sure its worth it. You don't want to waste time and end up overqualified but still unemployed.

More Satisfying Work

According to nearly a decade of research, reports state that over ninety five percent of workers in the United States of America are in the wrong roles. Further studies state that over seventy percent of American workers are not engaged at their jobs and over eighty percent don't like their jobs. Considering that the average American works eight hours every day, it's no surprise that people have difficulty waking up let alone enjoy their work. So why can't people find jobs they love? And how do they find jobs they love?

If your looking to stay on the employment circuit then now is the time to evaluate your options. At the end of the day your job should make you feel happy and at the same time it needs to make enough money for your life. Finding the right balance is the key. The triangle of happiness, money and passion is where you dream job lies.

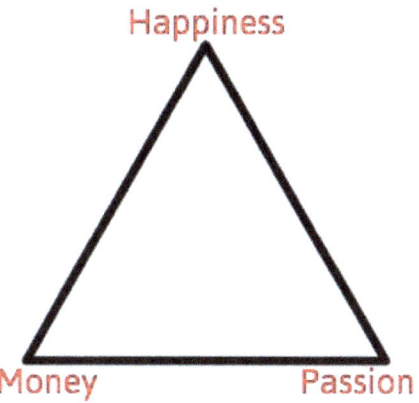

When you're looking for new opportunities in your chosen area of passion it's important to first of all improve your marketability. Find out what the key skills are in that field. Work on improving them. Maybe that involves going back to study or spending your free time learning. Use the chapter before to help you if necessary. When you boost those specific skills it will help you find work that your passionate about. In addition to those skills you should work on strengthening universal skills. These skills will help you with just about any career and most of them will come in useful for everyday life. Universal skills include things such as:

- Writing - Being able to express yourself with the written word is an essential requirement of most companies working in communications.

- Public speaking - If your good at speaking in front of groups of people then your good at motivating people. This provides a lot of value to companies.
- Negotiation - Good negotiation skills will help you and your employer. They can be used to increase your salary or complete successful business deals.
- Follow-up and follow-through - Any job you do will require commitment and persistence. Those who can face the challenges and ride through them provide the most value.
- Technology- Keep and stay up to date with technology in your industry and you will always be in demand.

Your Network is Your Networth

Did you know that over seventy five percent of jobs are not advertised? Regardless of what the media says about the lack of jobs there are more than enough opportunities being made available everyday. But finding them is going to require you taking responsibility beyond the standard jobs boards and employment agencies. It's going to require you to go out there and connect with people.

Power and security is in the connections you have. Knowledge and experience will only take you so far, people will complete the journey. Any job or income can stop at any time. The thing that will bring you back everytime is people.

'The richest people in the world look for and build networks; everyone else looks for work.' Robert Kiyosaki

The top business leaders will agree that your network is your net worth. We are all connected by roughly six degrees of separation. Everyone you come across can provide value to you. Regardless of whether they are in your industry or not. In the long run they could lead you to other people.. People outside of your industry will expose you to new ideas and new ways of thinking that will refresh your outlook.

Trust and respect should be the foundations of your relationships. When people see these qualities in you then they will be more likely to think of you when an opportunity arises. One of the best ways to form these bonds is to connect people with other people of value to them. The person will be flattered, grateful and remember you for helping them out.

Focus on building a connection with people you come across. Look for shared interests or passions. Put yourself out there. Attend seminars, conferences, meetings and activities that will put you into contact with other like minded people. In time you will start to build a solid network of high achievers. People will trust you much more when meeting you in person as opposed to cold calling or email.

If your going to meetings and networking events then prepare in advance. Have your business cards ready. Have an elevator pitch ready that describes who you are and your goals within a short period of time. Know what you plan to discuss beforehand. Dress the part, show up early and exude confidence. The busiest people will often show up early and you want to catch them. knowing beforehand what you want to discuss and who you want to meet. After the events its important to follow-up not only with new relationships, but also with those you have met before. You could send a simple email or some article on a topic you talked about.

It takes time and effort to build a network. You won't see the benefits right away but long term they will pay off. Develop existing relationships as well as meeting new people. Meet up with people for a coffee or share information and contacts. Tell them about your job search and they might be able to help. In return try to help whenever the opportunity arises. If they need information or connections share it. That should come naturally. It's all about adding value to that relationship in a personal way. A great book you can check out is How to Win Friends and Influence People by Dale Carnegie. This is a timeless classic on building connections. Or Never Eat Alone by Keith Ferrazi.

The Job Search

Start your job search by identifying thirty to forty companies. Prepare your resume and a cover letter. Send it to them. But don't stop there. You need to be aggressive and make personal contacts. Most companies won't hire you based only on seeing your resume. To make it happen you need to get into contact with the decision makers. Visit the offices, make phone calls and get in touch. Again it's all about the people. Don't sit at home waiting for a reply. Take action because if you get out there and hit up those businesses then it will make you a better connecter and bring you closer to securing a job. Keep going and expanding your network.

Interview

Normally when an employer is interested in you they will first offer you an interview. Once you have secured an interview it's wise to spend some time preparing for it. In that interview you will need to make a great first impression because there will be no second chances. Set aside time to do the following:

Research Before The Interview

Before you attend any interview you need to research key information about the company you're going to be interviewing at. This will give you more confidence when you go in for your interview. It's easy to find the basic information from the company's website or by doing a quick search online.

Then you can start to match up your skills with their vision. You will also know all about the companies developments and history which you can discuss and show interest in.

- *Prepare answers to common questions.*

Always have some default answers to questions that you think they will ask during the interview. These will be the generic questions such as "tell us about your last job" or "what will you bring to the company'. Be prepared for anything you think they might ask you. You will then appear more collected, confident and intelligent. If it helps then practice beforehand with a friend.

In addition have questions to ask your interviewers because they will always ask you if you have any questions. It shows your enthusiasm if you do have any. In fact they will expect you to ask questions if your thinking seriously about working there. Here are some good examples of questions you could ask them.

"Can you explain some of the daily duties of this job?"
"What are the best characteristics for this job?"
"How do you measure performance and how often?"
"What departments will I be working with and how do these departments communicate"
"What are the main challenges of this role?"

- *Re-read the job description*

You really need to have the job description clear and rehearsed in your mind. Print it out if it helps and underline the parts that you believe are linked to your strengths. Consider examples from your past experiences and skills that match to the position. The interviewer will likely also have a copy of this during the interview. Make sure your on the same page.

- *Prepare a list of references*

For sure your interviewers will require you to prepare a list of references before and or after your interview. Having these prepared in advance will give you extra kudos. Prepare in advance and contact your former employer to request their blessings. Which is why it's always a great strategy to leave your former employer on good terms.

Depending on the position that your applying for you might need to show examples of your work. Have those prepared and ready for the interview. Think of your best examples and discuss them with confidence.

Tips for during the interview

So you've spent some time preparing. Now to be successful on the interview day here are some tips.

- *First impressions*

First impressions is all about conveying confidence. Make eye contact, have a firm handshake and sit or stand straight. Remember that first impressions make a huge impact so make sure you dress well. Shine your shoes, put on a suit and arrive early. If you have never been there before, plan your route well in advance to avoid delays. When you arrive be respectful to everyone you meet. You never know who has influence and power there.

- *Rapport*

Good communication skills are crucial to a successful interview. The most important thing is to be a good listener. Focus on the information they give you. Allow them time to speak and never talk over them. Match their style and pace of talking to gain better rapport with them. Keep it professional and focus on the business. It's good to give away some personal interests and connect on those but don't digress too much.

In addition use appropriate language, no slang or lazy talk. When they ask you questions take the time to pause and then come up with an elaborative answer.

Always take the opportunity to prove your worth and be honest in your answers. If they focus on your weaknesses then steer it back to your strengths. Frame everything in a positive way, including any failures or weaknesses. Keep your answers concise and to the point. Also remember to ask them any questions you have prepared.

- *Bring copies of your resume, a notebook and pen*

It's a very professional approach to bring copies of your printed resume. Interviewers will appreciate your efforts and it will keep you in their mind. Highlight any important areas to discuss with them. Furthermore bring a pen and paper so you can take notes and jot down any questions you may have as the interview progresses. Again this is going to make you look more professional.

Tips for after the interview

After the interview you need to keep increasing your chances of success. Inquire about what you should do next. If they suggest a follow up email then start the email chain after the interview. By default you should always send a thank you email. Make sure you ask for any business card or their contact information. If there is an assignment then get right to it whilst the information is still fresh in your mind.

After you have finished the interviewing process and hopefully if they like you then you can start to think about negotiation. Never do this during the interview. It should come later on.

Ideally talk about it when your value is at its highest. When it comes to salary negotiation the biggest mistake people make is talking about money too early on. This advice also applies to people currently in positions that are looking to negotiate better terms. This is after they have attested to that through knowing more about you. If they terms weren't stated exactly then you can negotiate some better ones. Usually this is done in a second interview over the phone or in person if possible.

Most jobs will have a range of flexibility in what they pay. Plus most will have various other benefits such as housing, transport or health insurance. These are all very important. Negotiation is about coming together to make an initial agreement for payment of services. Both you and the employer should be happy with the result. You want to get paid fairly for your value whilst the employer doesn't want to overpay you. If the employer overpays then they will expect much more of you. Make sure you are aware and prepared for that. After all this isn't about you selling a product, it's about you joining a team. This is a win win situation if you both accept.

To make a solid case for a higher salary, you need to know your value and how to convey it. Bring up past and present evidence that proves you're worth. For example, instances where you helped the company to increase profitability for example, or reduce costs. Or maybe it was something that saved time and showed you as a credible performer. Be calm and confident when you talk about this.

Whilst knowing your value is really important, equally important is market research. you need to know what the current market rate is for paying someone with your qualifications and experience. Most of this information can be found online or by talking to recruiters. Remember that information found online also need to be relevant to your specific region. Additionally you can find out by asking people working in similar job titles to you.

When negotiating most people will give a range and not a specific number. This is a mistake because first of all the employer will likely go for the lower range. It also makes you look weak because your not being bold enough to state your true value. Better is too really know what it is that you want and state it. In your mind of course you will have your ideal and willing to settle number. Just make sure your happy with both. The ideal number should be slightly higher than what you'd normally expect for someone at your level. whilst the "willing to settle" will be a figure that you know is justifiable.

Make sure you have other options to leverage your chances. Always come from a place of abundance. Let the employer know that your considering other options and that will raise your value in their eyes. You can simply say to them that your considering multiple offers at the moment. This will enhance the 'scarcity' mentality in their minds. However if your negotiating at your current company then it might hurt you to to bring up the fact that you've received other job offers. Instead just say that this is the current market rate. Again explain your value and highlight your achievements.

When you negotiate salary timing is everything. Bringing it out of the blue isn't going to help much. If your in a new job offer situation then it's a good idea to only bring it up when your asked. If you bring it up it right away then it will make you look money hungry and not focused on adding value to the company through your actual work. If you're looking for a raise from your current company again timing is everything. The best time would be during any performance review time such as towards the year end. Managers will expect this more and you can highlight your highs from the performance review. Always be humble and polite, yet confident. If you have positive intentions of adding value then it will increase your chances of success.

Assuming you want the job but your sticking on the financial details then you could offer up some suggestions to trade them back for other things. That could be for example trading salary for vacation days or stock. There are many options of things which can be traded and offered up. Take your time, but don't get lost in pennies and details. They will want quick and affirmative decisions. Have a set date to make that decision for both you and the new employer. Then it's time to sign the contract and start a new job that you have always wanted. But if that's not the path for you then find out more about starting a business or travelling the world in the next chapters.

Build Your Dream Business

Perhaps the idea of being an employee is not for you. Perhaps instead your looking to pursue the entrepreneur/employer route. In that regard, setting up your business requires a solid goal and the plans to back it up. Having a business might look great but it comes at a price. However if you have the mindset and are prepared for what it takes then go for it. This chapter will help you to get going.

Modern technology and the internet have allowed people to easily start various kinds of businesses from anywhere in the world. Nowadays all you need is a laptop and an internet connection. Although starting a business is not something that comes with ease. Just ask any entrepreneur or small business owner. Sure you might have an idea but an idea doesn't become a profitable business without focused and consistent effort. There are a number of steps required to launch a business venture. But if you're willing to work hard then you can make a successful business. Let's go through some of the steps.

Evaluation

To begin with, we need to ask ourselves some basic questions. What are your reasons for wanting to start a business?

Focusing on the why is a good way to know whether launching a business is for you or not. That could be to meet a particular need in the marketplace, a problem to solve or to serve a personal need. The answers you come up with will help you to decide on the type of business you decide to start. If your just looking for some extra cash then maybe starting a side hustle would be a better idea. But if you are looking for more freedom then maybe you should think about starting a new business. With the reasons written down ask yourself some more evaluation questions. When you have found your reasons, keep asking yourself more questions to help you determine exactly the type of business you want to start, and to find out if you have what it takes. Don't censor your answers, be as honest as possible because this will create a foundation for everything you do moving forward. Consider the following questions.

- What are your skills?
- What are you passionate about?
- What is your speciality?
- How much do you need?
- How much do you have saved?

Ideas

Is there a business idea that you already have? If you do, go ahead and proceed to the next section. Otherwise use the following methods to brainstorm some fresh ideas. When you are coming up with new ideas run them by people. Seek advice from peers, mentors and other entrepreneurs. Here are some ideas to get you going:

- The future - What technology or changes do you see coming soon? Can you be ready and ahead of the market for the changes?
- Solutions - Do you have a fix to some common problems? If your business can fix an important problem then your customers will pay for the solution.
- Old skills to new fields - If you have been successful in one area try to shift that skillset or methodology to a new area.
- Be the best but for faster and/or cheaper - Focus on making a better service and adding more value for the best price and quickest results.
- Another option is to open a franchise of a company that is already established. Then your job is to find the location and secure sufficient funding.

Market research

Market research will bring clarity to your ideas and how you can monetize them. It will also help you to discover your target market, what they are missing and what they want. Are there other businesses doing what you're thinking about? Start your research on the competition. Inevitably you will come up with new and improved solutions which will result in you producing a higher quality product or service.

Don't neglect market research. Not doing so would be like driving with your eyes closed. When your driving you need to know your direction and what speed to go. It's the most important part to tell you what the demand is and to identify the competition. In the end this will reveal whether an idea is profitable enough or if maybe the stakes are too high. It will also reveal to you the buying habits of your customers, price points and much more. Here are the most fundamental market research methods for you start with.

Primary Research

Primary research involves collecting sales data and reviewing current practices and how effective they are. This is focused on your competition. Collecting primary research consists of:

- Interviews (telephone or in person)
- Surveys
- Questionnaires
- Focus groups consisting of potential customers or clients

Important questions can include:

- When purchasing this type of product or service what are the kind of things you might consider?
- What are the kind of things you like or don't like about the current products or services?
- Are there any areas that could be improved?
- What would be a suitable price for the product or service?

Secondary Research

Secondary research involves analyzing data that is publicly available. This data can be used to identify competitors, standards and customer targets. To succeed in business you need to fully understand your customers along with any suitable products and services. Customer targets usually consist of demographics, age, income and so on. List down all of the following.

- Customers - Who are your customers? Who will buy your product or service?
    - What age are they?
    - What is their background and income, etc.
- Products - What products do your competitors sell and at what price?
- Services - What services do your competitors sell and at what price?

- Marketing - How do your competitors generate business?
    - Are they using advertising?

When conducting market research, avoid the following common mistakes.
- Using only secondary research - Relying solely on the work of others will not give you the full picture. Sure it's a good starting point but often it can be outdated and you will miss other critical factors.
- Using only online resources - A lot of data online is not accurate or it is out of date. Consider using library resources, college campus information or small business center information.
- Surveying only friends and family - Too many budding entrepreneurs will only interview their friends and family when conducting research. The problem with that is most of them will not give you accurate answers since they want to make you happy.

During the research phase it is important to look at all the details. At this stage it will become more clear if your passionate about it or if there's a market or not for your business idea. Otherwise go back to the drawing board to brainstorm more ideas.

Write a business plan

By now you should have a good business idea beginning taking formation. With that idea in mind, ideally on paper or in a document you need to define it more. Begin with defining the purpose of the business. Who are you selling to? What are your end goals? How will you finance the business at the stat? The answers to these can be formulated in a business plan.

A business plan is a written document consisting of how your business will start and proceed to the final product. Most plans can cover everything required within twenty to thirty pages plus appendices for projections and other details. Anything more needs to be summarized better and anything less is lacking in important details.

Most new business entrepreneurs tend to rush into business without doing proper research and planning. Having a solid business plan will help you to figure out where your company is going, how it will overcome any obstacles and what you need to sustain it. Writing and creating a business plan is similar to creating a map for traveling. It needs to be clear and concise so that your people can easily follow it through the steps whilst you are developing your business. Ultimately this will navigate your business towards success. With a great plan that consists of where to go and how to do it, will a business owner and their team know if they are on the pathway to success.

If you have completed the market research then your well on your way because that takes up a huge part of the business plan. In addition to market research you need to think about the things that could go wrong. Just as we did with the fear setting exercise earlier on we need to also have an exit strategy in the event that things might go wrong.

If you have employees then share the plan with them. A business plan should not be hidden. The business plan serves to keep the company focused and it needs to be shared with everyone so that if necessary it can discussed and improved. Every worker or partners input should be considered so that the outcome is something that's pleasant to all.

Now a business plan doesn't need to be an elaborate multi page document that takes months to create. All you need is something that is easy to understand, and specific enough to cover all areas of concern. At the least it can include pictures, infographics and details for reference later on to ensure that the business is headed in the right direction towards meeting its goals. A good business plan should include the following.

- Title page - Begin with your business name. Before you start selling your product or service, you need a brand. Create a logo and name that can help people easily identify with your business. Then you can use this consistently across all of your platforms.

- Executive summary - This is a concise summary of what is inside the business plan. It will include the company description, the problem the business is solving along with the solution and why now. Detail the industry you wish to work in, how and why you intend to succeed.
- Business description - Outline the kind of business which you are going to start and what the current industry looks like. Plus include what it could look like in the future.
- Market strategy - Outline your target market, and how you plan to sell to that market. Include primary and secondary market research.
- Competitor analysis - Detail the strengths and weaknesses of your competitors. How will you beat them? Identify opportunities, threats and analysis of the current market.
- Company SWOT - Analyze your own strengths, weaknesses and identify any opportunities for growth. Plus identify any threats that might become obstacles.
- Development plan - Detail your product or service and how you will develop it. Include a budget for that product or service.
- Operations and management plan - How will the business function on a daily to yearly basis?

- Finances - Consider costs and projections for projects and stages. Where will the money come from? When?
- Exit strategy - Potential obstacles and how to overcome them

For each point, you can use between one to three pages. Remember that the business plan will evolve as your business matures. Keep updating it.

Staff

Hiring a great team will speed up your business success. If you have partners that's great too. Look for any of the gaps you need to fill in your business and find people to fit them. You shouldn't try to do everything yourself. Free up your time for the big things and get specialists to focus on the areas of expertise. Define their roles and responsibilities. Whether you are looking for a partner, an employee or even a freelancer, the following tips will help you to identify the best candidates.

- Clear goals - Make sure that everyone understands their role and the company vision form the very beginning.
- Hiring - When you are in the process of hiring you need to consider a number of different things. Make sure you screen them and ask the appropriate questions.
- Company culture - A healthy culture is all about respect and empowerment of employees. This can be achieved

through activities, including training and mentorship along with a positive atmosphere.

When your plan is finished keep it available for use. Again for the whole company. The plan is there for a reason and you can refer to it as much as possible. Just like a map keep referring to it to make sure that you're going the correct way.

Feedback

With your business plan in place you should by now have some kind of product or service. Now is the time to let people test your product or service and get their feedback. A fresh perspective will help identify any problems you might have missed. Plus these people can be your early supporters or review team. Every time you have a new service or product use this team to constantly improve and make sure you stay relevant. Keep in mind that some of that advice will be good whilst some of it won't be. Take the time to carefully consider all feedback. Be grateful for it and also seek the truth in it. Make a note of the times when things occur frequently and address them accordingly. If you keep hearing the same comments, then it's time to do something about it.

Finance

Launching any business comes with costs and you will need to make plans for how you will cover them. Do you have enough funds to get you going or will you need to borrow some? If you're planning to quit your job now to focus on your business, do you have enough money saved to take care of yourself and the business costs until you start making some money back?

One of the main reasons that startup businesses fail is because of funds running out before the business turns a profit. This can be heartbreaking when your so close. Therefore it's crucial to have enough finances covered and to always overestimate how much startup capital you will need. Furthermore keep your costs low when starting a business. Don't waste your money on expensive new equipment or luxuries that don't add significant value to your business goals. Be frugal when you start, only the essentials should be taken care of. When you grow and make profits then you can spend more on some luxuries.

In case you don't have enough funds at the beginning you can start out with a commercial bank loan. These can be difficult to secure but you can try through the Small Business Administration (SBA) or through another lender. Alternatively you may want to consider an investor. They can provide enough start up capital in return for shares or decisive power in your business. Crowdfunding is another way to raise many small amounts from numerous investors. There are a number of reliable crowdfunding platforms that have helped many startup businesses in recent years.

Overall there are many different ways to start your business should you require financial help. Take a look at the list below and consider your own resources and circumstances to decide which is the best fit for you.

- Funded by you - This might be difficult and take longer, but the upside is that you have more control and in turn more profit in your pocket.
- Friends and family - This can put a strain on relationships so be clear and set up the right conditions. Make it is as straightforward as possible.
- Request a small-business grant - Take a loot at Grants.gov. This is a searchable, online directory of over 1,000 federal grant programs. The best part is that it won't cost you any equity.
- Crowdfunding campaign - Many small investments can add up to something significant. There are so many crowdfunding options, check out Kickstarter, Indiegogo or do a Google search for the best options now.

- Apply to local angel investor groups - Get connected with your local business network to find potential investors or use online platforms such as Gust and AngelList.
- Venture capital investors (VCs) - VCs are always looking for the next big opportunity. They will have large sums to invest so make sure you business prospects are really great before approaching them.
- Startup incubator or accelerator - These companies are there help new businesses starting out. Many of them will offer free resources such as office space, consulting, and the right business connections.
- Negotiate an advance - If you have customers or partners already interested in your business and they are enthusiastic about it there's a chance they'll help fund it, too. Discuss an advance or investment with them.
- Trade equity or services - If you have services then you can offer them for free in exchange for investment in your company. Or maybe you can offer them shares. This should help you starting out.
- Bank loan or line of credit - If you meet the requirements, a good place to start for loan opportunities is the Small Business Administration.

Determine your legal business structure

Before registering a company, you first need to determine what kind of entity it is. Business structure will affect everything from filing taxes to your personal liability in the event that something goes wrong. Let's take a look at some of the most common business structures.

Sole proprietorship

When a business is entirely owned by yourself and you are the one who is responsible for all obligations and any debts then you can register as a sole proprietorship. It's important to note that this structure will directly affect your personal credit.

Partnership

Businesses can be a great success when you work with someone who has complementary skills to your own. When two or more persons are counted liable as owners of the business it is known as a partnership.

If you decide to have your personal liability separate from your company's liability then forming one of several types of corporations will help you. In the event that someone tries to sue you then you can protect your personal finances.

Limited liability corporation (LLC)

The LLC is one of the most popular options for a small business. This has all the legal protections of a corporation and also has the tax advantages of a partnership.

C-corporation

C-corporations are suitable for businesses which plan to go public or seek funding from venture capitalists in the near future.

Ultimately, it is up to you to decide the best type of entity for your current needs and future business goals. If you are having difficulty to make up your mind or your confused then it would be a good idea to discuss the decision with a business or legal adviser.

Becoming Official

Registering with the government and the IRS is a step you have to take to be recognized as an official business entity. All corporations require an "articles of incorporation" document. This must include the name of your business, it's purpose, stock details, corporate structure and any other information requested by them about your company. Alternatively you can just register your business name and trademark your business name in case you want to protect that name.

Once your business has been registered you will need to apply for an employer identification number (EIN) from the IRS. However if your operating as a Sole Proprietorships with no staff then this will not required. Although it might be a good idea to apply for one anyway because it will keep your personal and business taxes separate. In addition, this will keep things open if you decide to hire people later on. To get a free EIN you can register on the IRS website.

There will also be other forms that you have to file to fulfill the federal and state income tax requirements. These are dependent on your business structure. Hire a lawyer or accountant to help you with this. Most firms will offer a full service and take care of everything for the whole year on your behalf.

Insurance

Purchasing business insurance is an important step to take and you shouldn't procrastinate the decision. Get it from the start or before your business is operating. This will cover you in the event of theft, damage or even a lawsuit. If you are going to employ people at the least you will have to purchase workers' compensation in addition to unemployment insurance. Depending on your location and industry it might be required for you to have other types of additional insurance. General liability (GL) insurance, or a business owner's policy is the best option for most small businesses. This will cover damages to property and any injuries to yourself or others involved. If your business provides a service then professional liability insurance is the best option. In the event that of any wrongdoing or neglecting to do something that you should then it will cover you.

Location

The location and facilities of your business will differ depending on your needs. Here are some things to consider.

- Style of operation - Make sure your location is consistent with the style and image of your business. Also, make sure that your easy to find. Do you need to rent a building? Or can you use office spaces?
- Demographic - Consider who your customers are, is important to be near them? Are there competitors nearby? Sometimes this can be a good thing, other times, it's not. By now you should know which is best for your business.

Coworking spaces

Coworking is the latest trend in the fast moving modern workplace. Many companies, startups and entrepreneurs are using cowing spaces to run their businesses from. Working in these environments is reported to positively influence their lives and work by putting them into contact with other like minded individuals as opposed to working at home or in a coffee shop. Most say it makes them more creative, confident and happy being around people. Office settings tend to be a bit too dry and confined. Whilst coworking spaces usually have a more modern environment with places to work, relax and eat. Most also offer free coffee!

Overall it's better for your mental health to have a routine of going somewhere to work and being around other people. Avoid isolating yourself. You will need a healthy amount of positive self esteem to reach your goals. Being around the right people is a major benefit.

There are so many coworking optionsavailavle these days. From the simple renting a desk to a whole office for your team. They will usually offer daily rates or monthly and longer term plans.

Grow your business

To run a successful business, you need a growth mindset. Profit and success depend on growing your business. This will take time and effort, but what you put into it you will get back.

Collaboration with more established businesses in your industry is one of the most effective ways to achieve growth. Through your earlier research you should have a list of other companies or influential people who can approach for some promotion or collaboration. There are many, many methods to grow your business. For example you could target a new market, acquire another business, expand your products or services and much more. At the very least you need to take care of two key components of successful growth that all burgeoning companies have in common.

First of all they have an effective marketing plan. This comes via social media marketing or paid advertising campaigns. Through this they know exactly who to target both online and offline. Once customers have been found they are well aware of how to keep them. After all the easiest way to sell to is to a customer you have already sold too because they will have already committed to your products or tested what you have. Through the process they have started a relationship with your business. It is your duty to keep the relationship happy and make them feel good and add value. In business you will always need to compete for these kinds of customers so you always need to take care of them and add value. In addition you need to continually research the marketplace, hire the best people and keep on improving your products or services.

Things will go wrong and obstacles will arise along the way. Always be prepared to adjust. You might have the best plan but when its in action things will change. Always be solutions focused on finding new ways forward and to continue growing even through the challenging times.

There are millions of sales strategies and techniques. Begin with identifying potential customers who would want to use or buy your products or services. Advertise and find customers who are perfect for your business. Then design and implement the most effective sales funnel and strategy that will convert these leads into money. To help you keep it simple here are four things to keep in mind.

1. Listen - Listen to your clients or customers and they will tell you what they want and need, and how to make that happen.
2. Ask for a commitment - Never be shy to take a step forward and close a sale or upsell. Just don't be pushy about it.
3. Don't be afraid of rejection - Even if one customer declines your offer don't be put off. Improve, learn and move forward.
4. Prioritize Revenue & running a profitable business - Focus on the things that make a difference.

Lifestyle Design

Whether your dream is to travel through rural China and run an online publishing business. Or to travel across South America on a motorcycle learning Spanish and sourcing products for clients, the most important part is to have a vision. This comes from you and that is regardless of what others think.

Designing your lifestyle will give you the control to live how you want, when you want and wherever you want. Maybe you want to spend a few months overseas and then a few months in your home country. Or maybe you want to spend an indefinite amount of time in a specific country. Then again you could become a perpetual traveller with no permanent home, living out of your suitcase. Travelling from country to country.

Map out what your perfect day would be like. Go into it in detail. What time would you wake up? Where would you be living? How much time would you spend working? How would you spend the rest of your day? Compare that with how your spending your days now. Be clear on what you don't want. That could be not having to get up at a certain time or to not having a boss to answer to. List all of it down.

Take a moment to ask yourself, am I where i want to be? Be clear on this intention. Having an idea to just "go somewhere" is not enough. That would be like getting into a car and saying "just drive". Instead when you decide where you want to go a map will appear and you will get to your destination much faster. If your not living where you want to at the moment then you need to start making moves to get there.

That could be anything from a family vacation to Australia, backpacking India or volunteering in South America. Next you need to make a plan and set a deadline. Then ultimately you need to take action without procrastination. You can have all that knowledge and the best plans but action is the most important step. A good plan without action is useless.

Once you have clearly defined your wants and not wants you can create a vision board. This can include pictures of all the things of significance to your dreams. Put them all on a board and hang it somewhere you will see everyday. This will tap into your subconscious and help you to turn your dreams into reality. But imagination is not enough on its own. We also need to take consistent daily actions towards our goals. Define what actions are necessary to making your dream lifestyle possible. Break down them down into chunks as we discussed before. Having an actionable strategy will allow you to make massive progress in your life. Keep moving forwards and taking actions towards making it happen. Avoid staying still and getting caught up in the planning and procrastination. People will be attracted by the fact that you're taking action, and in turn more opportunities will come your way.

For most of us, traveling is a dream that we never fulfill. From excuses to fears to the costs. We end up procrastinating on doing what we really want to. Now for some of us living overseas might be more difficult, especially if you are married or have children. However it's still possible so don't be put off by that. At the start it might be difficult but once you get going it will become much easier. If you have a family or are tied into a job then you can still plan some trips here and there with proper budgeting and time management in place. The best way in that regard would be to save in advance. Also it can be done whilst working full time if you use your and your partners holidays wisely.

But what if you don't have enough money or any location independent work but you still want to travel for longer periods of time? Yes, long term travelling can be expensive but it doesn't have to be. In fact there are some really cost effective solutions out there available, even if you have a family traveling with you. Some options are even paid. Let's take a look at some of the things you can do for long term travelling.

Start with the financial side of things. How much is it going to cost you to live your ideal life? Do you have enough saved to sustain a year or more? Will your business bring in enough cash? Start by figuring out your expenses. How much do you spend daily? Figure out all the small things like bills, toiletries, food, trips, investments and so on. If you aren't already doing this. Start doing it now. Keep everything in an excel sheet and get yourself a good expenses tracking application. Most of us in the world are living in debt and we spend way too much money on material things. Instead of wasting money on these things which are old after a few weeks, why not put it towards a memorable lifetime experience. Are you really more fond of your designer shoes over your best holiday memories? Spend money on experiences, not materialism.

Travelling the World

Make it happen and go see the world. It can be an enlightening experience to see how other cultures live or the natural beauty of the world. Travelling the world for extended periods of time is not only for the wealthy. In fact, anyone can do it and usually the only one stopping you, is you.

So how much money do you really need to travel the world? Well that all depends on how long your planning on going for and where you're going. A year long trip around the world is going to cost you roughly $20,000. That includes time in both expensive and cheap countries. Now that does sound like a lot but just think about how much you are spending in a year right now. There are so many small expenses that you need to be aware of such as daily spending, food, transport and more.

Next is to make your plans as cost effective as possible. Look into booking flights as far in advance as possible. Also take into consideration the actual days you will be flying on. Be flexible about your time of travel and it will allow you to make some savings. There are multiple search engines you can use for booking flights. Compare them against each other. I suggest, Google Flights, Skyscanner and Budget Flights. You can also follow travel companies and airlines on social media to stay up to date with the best deals they offer. Weekdays tend to be much cheaper, particularly Tuesdays and Thursdays. To save more if possible you could take a bus trip across countries, it will save you plenty of cash and make for an interesting ride. In fact there are many overnight buses available around the world.

When it comes to accommodation hostels and guest houses offer the best prices. Plenty of other travellers do this so it's also a fun way to make new friends. A few years ago I stayed at hostels in downtown Hollywood. During my time there I was invited to some really cool parties and met life long friends. In addition hostels will often have kitchens so you can save money through buying food and cooking your own or sharing with others. Alternatively in places like Asia the street food is really tasty and quite cheap. Trust me it is a much more memorable and fun experience than paying hundreds of dollars for a boring hotel room.

Make Money While Travelling the World

Now if cost really is a barrier for traveling then why not work whilst you travel? You could use some of the following ideas to make money online or you could work in the countries you visit. In fact it will probably make your experience much more fun because you will be put into contact with new friends and experiences that you probably wouldn't have encountered otherwise. Here are some ideas for working whilst travelling.

Travel Blogging

Travel blogging is a really fun job and obviously works perfectly with travelling. If you make it big then it can turn into a lucrative long term income stream. Start your travel blog right away. Regularly update it with your videos, images and notes on advice and experiences from wherever you go. When your following starts to grow then you can start to charge for advertising. You can also sell affiliate products or be a guest poster on another travel blog. There are so many ways to monetize this.

Volunteering

There are a number of popular volunteer programs available from six months and beyond. You can base yourself in some of the most far flung regions. Volunteering any of these organizations will introduce to places and people that you normally wouldn't see. They are available to a wide range of candidates. Most offer accommodation and food. Some even offer to pay travel expenses. Below are some of the most popular.

- The Peace Corps
- The United Nations
- Art Corps
- Geekcorps.org

Make Money Online

Nowadays it's easier than ever to make money online. Which means you can live and work location independent. This presents a wonderful opportunity for people to start earning a decent income online and results in amazing opportunities for wealth creation, freedom and entrepreneurship.

Remember that at the end of the day your focusing on freedom. If you quit your nine to five job to end up working twenty hours a day then it's not a smart move. You might not need to quit your job right away. Most of the make money online opportunities are very flexible and just require time spent. That time can be spent anytime of the day. We all need to start somewhere so check out some of the opportunities outlined in this chapter. Go with the one that resonates with you. Start small and work hard. None of this is get rich quick but if you put in the effort you will reap the rewards. The opportunities to make money online are abundant and incredibly varied to the skills required. Let's take a look at some of the best options right now.

Freelance

The modern job market is becoming much more remote. You don't really need to go to the office anymore because most work can be done online. Which means all you need is a laptop and wifi connection. If you have some tech and digital skills then you are likely to find some lucrative freelance work.

Sign up to some of the top jobs boards such as Flexjobs, upwork and freelancer. Everyday there are thousands of new jobs posted here from a diverse range of companies and positions. There is everything from graphic design to video editing to voice overs and much more.

Pay rates can vary a lot but if you have some good skills and experiences then it's going to be more valuable and worth more to the client. Make sure you have a solid profile that outlines your experiences, skills and links to your work. Then keep upto date with identifying and applying for new opportunities.

Podcasting

Do you have a passion that you want to share with the world? Audio podcasts can be a great way to share your message and discuss the things which your passionate about. This method is becoming increasingly popular with more and more people creating their own podcasts. It costs nothing to produce them except the initial equipment costs plus some hosting space. Launching your own show will bring you closer to what you really are interested in. In return this will produce passionate results and people will follow that. All you need to do is choose a podcast hosting company like iTunes, YouTube or Spotify and then get creating.

Blog

A blog is pretty similar to a podcast in the sense that its providing information on a subject. Although obviously the medium of the message is different. So if you have a passion but prefer to write about it then blogging can be another great way to monetize your passions. As with podcasting you first need a niche. The more specific it is the better. Specific niches attract more advertisers and are easier to find for your customer base.

Getting started is easy, just use WordPress with a web hosting company and a domain service provider. Then you just need to start creating regular content and experimenting with advertising to attract people. It can take a long time to build a following but stick with it. Believing in what you do and being passionate about it will help

Rent out your stuff

Since your not using it 24/7 or you might be traveling then renting your stuff out can be a great money maker. That could be anything from the bike you don't use to your whole wardrobe. Check out www.Turo.com In addition you could rent out your home with www.Airbnb.com

Courses

If you have some valuable knowledge then you could help others to learn it whilst earning an income through the internet. Online courses are in demand these days and they aren't only limited to business subjects. Platforms such as teachable and udemy allow you to create a course on anything you want. Then you simply upload, market and sell it.

Consider your skills. Maybe you're an artist or your skilled at marketing. Come up with a framework of how you can teach that skill. The cameras on smartphones these days are more than adequate enough to film the content. In most courses some slides and speaking to the camera will be enough. As long as the content is great and offers value then people will buy it.

The best thing about selling courses online is that it's completely passive. Which means you do the work once. Upload it and then it sells whilst you get busy living life or creating more content. As you start to build a following around your course you can market and upsell extra benefits such as coaching with your customers.

Ebooks

Ebooks are another form of passive income. Not only that but they open up to many more ways of making money. Simply find a subject and research its profitably. Now you will need to study more on this in order to get a better understanding of how to analyze the market. However, the learning curve is quite quick.

Amazon KDP (Kindle Direct Publishing) allows you to easily publish a book and start selling it on Amazon. Once you have an ebook uploaded you can further monetize it in paperback and audiobook formats. Plus you can sell across a bunch of different online stores. Again like making courses you can start to engage with your customers and then upsell them other products of yours.

If you write your own books then you can also start to sell your services as a writer. Copywriting, article writing and content writing is in demand on a huge scale. Some people even want guest posts on their blogs. This can be lucrative and also send even more traffic your way. All for doing something you're passionate about. the better your content becomes, the more money you will make.

Investment

Perhaps you have some money to invest but not much time. A powerful way forward is to make your money work for you. Investing doesn't have to be complicated or risky. There are some great advances in technology which have made it much safer and easier. Check out The Robinhood app which allows you to easily choose stocks, options, EFTs and cryptocurrencies to invest in. The best part is you don't pay any commissions or fees which is usually the case when done through a broker.

If your investing in stocks, focus on the index funds because they offer a diverse investment range across the market. That means you will have shares in a large number of the biggest companies in the US. Therefore you have more chances to profit. For further diversify you should choose international companies to invest into as well. Then if your interested in being a more active trader, check out FOREX for global trading options.

Remember that when investing you need to think long term. This isn't a get rich thing so don't worry about short term fluctuations. Focus on the long term investment. Investing in a diverse range of stocks will help you ride out any storms.

Coding and app development

Are you good with coding? If you are then realize that the world is moving more and more towards artificial intelligence and digital technology. This opens up massive opportunities for those with the right experience. If your working for a company doing this then you might be better off going your own way.

Amazon currently have a Developer Rewards program to pay coders for developing for Alexa. Plus if you want to build a business coding then post a portfolio on sites like Fiverr and UpWork to generate some business.

Maybe you have a great idea for an app. Or a company is looking for developers. Its no secret that there is a lot of money to be made in app development. There are loads of different types of apps and the future looks strong for the technology. Then there are multiple ways to generate income from them. Including advertising, affiliate links, subscriptions and more.

Video and Pictures

Video is becoming the most popular formats. According to Cisco, by 2022, it will account for over eighty percent of all internet traffic. Advancements in video technology are creating amazing opportunities to make money online.

If you have an eye for catching great content then upload it to a site such as Shutterstock. Then you can sell them there. Make use of your skills. Then use the money you make to invest into better equipment such as drones. Real estate companies always need these kind of images.

Membership site

When you become an authority figure online people are going to start to want more from you. Membership sites are a great way to create a consistent income and consistently add value to your customers.

With a membership site the members will have access to exclusive content in exchange for a subscription fee. This is usually paid on a monthly basis. The longer you can continue to provide valuable content to your members the happier they will be to stay subscribed or join.

This is another great form of passive income since you create the content once and it is consumed forever by your members. Good ideas for exclusive content are weekly webinars, coaching calls, tools and digital content such as videos, audio or articles.

YouTube

YouTube has created many millionaires and superstars. This is a revolution in the entertainment industry. The power is now in the hands of the public. Before you had to rely on talent agencies and studios to help you. But now YouTube allows people to create unlimited content and monetize it.

To make it on YouTube will require passion and focus to fuel be making consistent and high quality videos. I won't lie, these days it's become really competitive. But if you find your angle, niche and way to produce the best content for it then you will be onto a winner.

Get up to date on the metrics that count. Pay attention to who is having success on YouTube and how their achieving it. Stick with it and keep creating content. You will improve.

Ecommerce

There are hundreds or thousands of opportunities right now to make money online through ecommerce. For example a drop-shipping business is easy to start and you don't need to hold any products. Or you can set up an FBA (Fulfilment By Amazon) account and start selling your own products. The same can be done with a Shopify store and sell there.

Affiliate marketing

Affiliate marketing a quick and inexpensive method of making money online without having to have a product. The process works by an affiliate earning a commission for marketing another person's or company's products. All the affiliate has to do is search for a product they enjoy, then promote it and earn a percentage of the profit from each sale they make. Sales are tracked via affiliate links. Affiliate marketing allows you to make money at any time, from anywhere, even while you sleep.

Since we are leading to the topic of money then ultimately we need to talk about Financial freedom.

Financial Freedom

The average age of retirement in the United States is sixty five years old. However, many of us are more interested to make that happen sooner. Retiring early might seem impossible to you but there are in fact many ways to become financially free and reach retirement long before your sixty plus. After all the main motivation for early retirement is to enjoy life outside of work. That could be traveling, spending time with your family, pursuing hobbies and so on. Tell me, wouldn't it be better to do that whilst your still young and healthy?

To start your journey to becoming financially free, you must first understand the mindset of the different economic classes. Distinguishing where people focus their financial attention will help you to decide where your focus goes.

- The Poor - Focus only on expenses. They are living paycheck to paycheck and always work for money. As a result they never get out of the rat race.
- The Middle Class - Focus on liabilities, buying more and getting into debt. Any investment usually guided by a financial planner. They also must continue to work for money and remain stuck.

- The Rich - Focus on asset acquirement and allowing their assets to pay for any of their liabilities and expenses. Their finances continue to compound and grow.

Most people get stuck in the rat race because of their financial commitments. Rent to pay, a mortgage to keep up with, bills to pay, expenses and so many other things tying them down. Having a job and a salary is a convenient and consistent way to stay in this trap. So how can you escape this? Well first of all it's not going to happen overnight. We need to get real here. But if your willing to do what it takes and dedicate yourself then you too can be financially free. Instead of having to work hard at something you don't like for the benefit of someone else you can do it for you.

Financial freedom means that you have enough savings, investments and cash to afford the lifestyle you want for you or both you and your family without having to work. Achieving financial freedom requires you to know exactly what those figures mean for you. Each person will have their own needs and so it's difficult to come up with a precise figure.

Typically savings for requirement are five to fifteen percent of a person's salary. The amount your able to increase those savings by will allow you to reach retirement much earlier. The question is, how can someone with a lower income retire just as quickly as someone with a higher income? For now cut back on things such as travel and instead take public transport. Spend less on groceries, eating out or luxury expenses. Instead of buying the latest designer brands find something that is a more cost effective alternative. Cancel any subscriptions that you rarely use such as Netflix or take away dinners. You will also free up time to focus on your side hustles/passion business. If your in an expensive place consider downsizing.

All of these things are society's way of keeping you locked in the rat race. Work hard and spend it all. But if you can take on some short term pain for long term gains then you will become more free. Retirement should ideally start when you are debt-free. Therefore you shouldnt be making any payments for a mortgage, credit cards, medical bills, student loans or any other debt. In the event that you are still paying off any debts, be sure to add those payments to your budget.

Make changes that will have the biggest impact. Housing, transport and food are the main expenses. Having a surplus of money first requires you to reduce your expenses. Here are some things to consider:

Housing:

Consider moving and finding a cheaper place. Or you could even move in with someone to help with the bills. Don't be ashamed to move in with friends or family for a short time whilst you build wealth.

Transportation:
Transport can cost a lot. Oftentimes we don't need some of the luxuries because its based on laziness. Of course you need to go places but public transport can be a cheaper alternative.

Food:
Food costs can add up to large sums without you knowing. Pay attention here. Get yourself an application to track spending. You will robably be shocked at how much you spend on food. Yes you can still eat out but pay attention to the daily habits and things you pay too much for. Do you really need to spend ten dollars on a coffee?

Insurance and health:
Shop around for the best insurance. Calculate your Dr and Dentist visits, toiletries and so on. Buy in bulk if you can.

Bills:
Get your bills down. If your on a phone contract then get out of it because most are ripping you off. Switch off the lights and turn things ogg when you go out.

TV:
Don't waste money on all the latest streaming services. Find one and stick with it. Not only will that reduce your expenses but it will also give you more time and focus for your business.

Utility Expenses:
Optimize your bills, phone bill, rent and so on.

Education:
Education is important. Factor in any courses you want to study, books to buy.

Family:
If you have a family add up school fees, spouse living costs and so on

Vacation:
We all need a vacation now and then. Calculate your number of vacations, average costs, frequency and so on.

Clothes:
We all need new clothes every now and then. Think about how much you need to spend each month on clothes. Save on luxuries.

Luxuries:
Add in all the material gifts, treats but don't go overboard.

Daily spending:
Food shopping, taxis, coffees, etc. Track these and look for ways to improve on them.

Finally add everything together to give you an idea of how much you'll need each month to achieve your ideal retirement lifestyle. Take your time to make it as accurate and as realistic as possible. It's better to over budget things. Once you have estimated your monthly expenses for retirement, the next step is to calculate how much money you need to make it happen. There are a number of ways to estimate this. The first way is to have between thirty five to forty times your expected yearly expenses. That's assuming you live until eighty five years old and want to retire at forty to fifty years old. Calculate your monthly expenses by twelve to give you a yearly estimate. Next, find your target range. For example.

Monthly expenses: $4500 x 12 = Yearly expenses: $54,000
Target: 54 x 35 = 1.89 million.
54 x 40 = 2.16 million.
Target range for retirement: **1.89 - 2.16 million**

Saving up to 2.16 million isn't going to be easy, especially if you want to make it happen quickly. This is the step where you need to be disciplined. Retiring early will require you to save much more of you income. Many people with the goal of early retirement live on less than fifty percent of their income. Plus they will take on extra work to earn more. At the minimum you should have enough to cover your expenses without working for three months. In fact everyone should have this amount relevant to them in their bank account at any given time. Without this you're setting yourself up for a trap because life can be incredibly unpredictable and it serves well to prepare for the worst case scenarios. This emergency fund will be there to cover you against the big costs that happen out of your planned control. Things such as the car breaking down or quitting your main job. Imagine having twelve months worth of this figure in your bank. Now that's when you start to really taste financial freedom.

Accounting and budgeting should be done a minimum of once a month. The time should be spent reviewing your spending for the month and to make plans for the future. Keep a track of everything you spend. There are a number of apps to help you with it. As you log the data you will start to see patterns, ways to save and better money management. This will help you figure out what you really need as opposed to wasted money. Have a budget and stick to it. You need to know where your money goes and then control it. Take advantage of the budgeting apps available right now to help you with the process. The more you earn and the less you spend now brings you closer to early retirement. Living paycheck to paycheck is a sure fire strategy for going broke.

Creating a budget might seem a little daunting but all it requires is a little bit of discipline and planning but the results are going to be well worth it. Priorities can change over time and that's fine. So one month you might spend more on travelling then clothes for example. When you have a budget it will really help you to focus on the things that matter and start to make massive progress towards financial freedom. Plus you will be able to make regular travels. In the early days of our plan we need to be able to live off of not a lot of money. Long term if your escape plan is to leave the rat race then for a period of time you will need to cut back on your finances. Minimize them as much as possible now so that later you can live from your savings. Now of course you can't get rid of everything and live like a stoic. That can work for a little while but it's going to be difficult to sustain. Instead make some careful lifestyle changes. At least for a period of time to get you on the way to financial freedom or early retirement.

A great financial strategy is to always pay yourself first. Any money you make pay off all your expenses with and also set aside a portion for yourself. It works well if you define a percentage of your income every month. Say ten to thirty percent. That money saved will keep growing as you invest it. Stay consistent with it. Eventually that will start to pay you back a full time wage and more.

Extra Income

Ultimately with your expenses reduced you now need to focus on earning more money because frugality will only get you so far. Plus you don't want to live a poor life forever. If you want to live free and in luxury then you have will have to earn more money. There are tons of money making endeavours that you can do independently to increase your income. Take a look at the earlier chapters for some good ideas. This is the hard part because at the start you probably won't have much time, clients or sales. Therefore it needs to run alongside your current job until it reaches the point where you can live from it. Don't expect a full time wage right away. It's going to take time, plus it's going to take trial and error.

Essentially you will be spending all of your time off of your main job working on your side hustle. It means you will need to give up your weekends to make it happen. The more time you give to it the more quickly you will succeed. As you start to grow the income you can eventually work less hours at your main job and then finally break free to do you own thing.

Now what exactly would your side hustle or passion business be? Well there are millions of different ways to make money. We have discussed many of those already so make sure you are moving ahead with them. But the most important thing as we touched on before is to choose something you actually enjoy. Because if you actually enjoy it then it won't feel like work and you will spend more time crushing it.

Brainstorm all the things that your really good at, the things you like and the things your passionate about. Don't censor yourself and don't think about money yet. Just write out a huge list of all those things. When you have your list you can start to research how people with similar interests have monetized their ideas. Let's take a look at some examples.

- Music - You could make music and sell it online or work as a freelancer.
- Fashion - You could resell or make your own on demand designs.
- Art - There are so many possibilities, from commissioned local projects to freelance services.

There is nothing stopping you from trying to make money in areas that interest you. We live in a modern world where that is very easy to do. Everyone is connected to the internet these days. Plus we have thriving local communities in the big cities. Start trying out your ideas. The only way you will learn what works is by trying it out. Don't worry about making mistakes the earlier you make them closer and quicker you can get to realizing your goals. Keep learning and find what works. When you find something that works you can start to build on it.

Investment Options

With all the money you save from living more frugally and earning extra money it will give you more options to invest. This is a long term option for generating more gains on your money. There are a number of ways to invest. Real estate, bonds, how to invest in real estate. With the right mindset, strong investment strategy and excellent side hustle you can easily escape achieve financial freedom.

Whilst having savings is good, even better is to make those savings work for you. By investing in stocks and assets you can increase your money saved and make it work for you.

One of the best investment options is to use is www.vanguard.com. This website allows you to mix your investment portfolio across mutual funds, stocks and bonds. On average you can get at least a return of around ten percent. Over the long run that will compound and increase your investment significantly. Even when there are dips in the market it won't matter if you have a long term vision. However please do your research before investing. At the bare minimum I suggest reading one personal finance book a year along with some podcasts.

Max Out Your Retirement Accounts

Whenever you plan to retire the most important thing is to start early and save frequently. Retirement accounts such as 401(k)s and IRAs are a great way to achieve this. Whilst you're still earning an income do your best to max out your retirement accounts. Take full advantage of the opportunity to contribute more. For those of you over the age of fifty you can contribute a $1,000 catch-up contribution each year.

If you have a 401(k) at work, you can contribute up to $19,000 a year for 2019, or $25,000 if you're age 50 or older. Those limits increase up to $19,500 and $26,000, respectively, for 2020. Make sure you invest enough to take full advantage of any match your employer offers. Essentially it's free money.

Assets

Building assets is one of the most important components of financial freedom. The traditional route people take in wealth creation is to trade time and effort for money. Basically this is an endless cycle and eventually you're going to run out of time. Assets will always keep producing income regardless of whether you are working or not. The fact is that if you want to be financially free then you need to make your money to work for you, otherwise you will be working for it for the rest of your life. Decide now to begin you financial education. Don't be put off by the steep learning curve. Yes, at the start it's going to require a lot of work without much reward, but eventually the education will start compounding. Soon enough your efforts will pay off financially.

The difference between this and what the wealthy do is that they build an asset and that asset generates money. They will be selling their assets or renting their asset and in exchange they'll be making money. The big difference is that they only have to spend the time once and the asset keeps making money. For example if you publish a book online or if you build apps and put them on an App Store then you will have online assets in place. Depending on demand and quality is how much you will generate in cash for them. That could also go on indefinitely. As long as that asset has value you will keep being paid for it.

The wealthy know that they cannot be at the same place all the time and so they build services or products which they can scale. Even better if they are passive. These are the kind of things that will sell on their own. For example look at what Jeff Bezos has done with Amazon. It is a highly scalable product and service which has made him a multi billionaire because he has many other people working on his behalf. Could you do something similar?

Changing your mindset is going to have a massive result in your business life. Start to reconsider focusing on asset building activities. By approaching it this way you will be leveraging your time.

Examples of assets and liabilities:
- A house = Asset, it is something that someone owns and that has a physical form. You can rent this out.
- Cash = Cash is a financial asset. You can use it to invest.
- Inventory = This is an asset, these are goods that we own, and intend to sell.
- A loan = This is a liability, since the company owes money.

Another valuable asset is established clientele. The rich have trusted partners and clients who will be more than happy to promote them and make referrals. This enables the rich to consistently grow their business. In return the rich have to continually make sure their clients are happy and that they are adding value to them.

The power comes in connections, rich people always have massive networks consisting of key people that help them to get to the next level. They can call upon them any time because those people are dedicated to their cause. This includes support from your family and friends. Now if you don't then it's time to move on and create it for yourself. Search for the right support. It doesn't matter where you start but what counts is that you reach up and you ask for help. Forget your pride and your ego. Go look for the people that are willing to help you and get rid of the people who are not helping you. The rich are always cultivating relationships and taking responsibility for moving them forward and adding value. Reputation is everything if you want to become wealthy through your business ventures.

It might sound obvious but it's true that money is an asset and you do need it to make money. However when starting out you can begin with capital from credit. You could for example apply for a loan or borrow money from someone that you trust. Start with what you have and grow it.

Work With a Financial Advisor

Finally, unless you have a financial background, it's a good idea to work with a trained financial advisor who has proven knowledge and experience. They will help you to develop an investment strategy making it easier for you to retire early. They will be able to show you exactly how much you need to invest each month to reach your goals within a certain number of years. Then when you retire they can help to manage your income streams so that they last. That income could come from dividends, Social Security, benefit plans, real estate investments and assets.

When seeking financial advice take your time to find people you get on well with. Because you will be working with them for a long time. Therefore it's important that you trust and like them. Cost shouldn't be the deciding factor. If you find the right advisor the value they add will be well worth the costs.

Many of us would love to retire early, but we often lack the financial resources, planning and discipline to do so. However it is indeed possible to retire early if you're willing to work hard and be smart. Remember to also consider the lifestyle of going from work to no work because it will be a serious lifestyle shift. You might get bored with all the free time. Just be aware of that and have a plan for how you will be living your new life. No one feels great after bingeing on Netflix for ten hours, especially when it's the sixth day in a row.

Staying Productivity Even if Your Lazy

Now whether your going to retire early, find a new job or start your own business it's crucial to make sure you stay productive and avoid laziness. The essence of productivity is not about working harder, it's just simply about doing less. It's about getting rid of time wasting activities and focusing on what you do best. Most people try to stuff as many things into their schedules and their to-do lists in an attempt to get as many things done as possible. But the truth is when you attempt to do too many things your time gets wasted because you're constantly switching between tasks instead of optimizing what tasks you should be working on. That's in fact how most people define working hard and getting things done. Sure you might make progress in lots of different things but when you get rid of all of these things and focus on only one thing instead you will go much further. For example if you have ten units of energy and you put it into ten different things you're going to make one unit of progress in each thing. But if you put ten units of energy into one thing you're going to make ten units of progress in it. The real secret is to do less.

Take a look at your life. Track where you spend each hour of the day. Do this exercise for at least one to two days a month. The main culprit of time wasted is personal things such as errands around the house. For example, cleaning, food shopping, deciding what to eat, cooking, eating, washing the dishes, checking the mail and so on. All of those are things that mostly waste time and that you need to either reduce or get someone else to do. When your making big money then it only makes sense for you to hire people to do this for you so that you can focus on the big projects. Even if your not making bags of money it will still be a great idea to outsource those time wasting tasks. Instead of spending time on washing and cooking you need to be spending time on your business. Alternatively what you could do for example is to batch those tasks together. So once a week you could do all your grocery shopping or prepare all your meals for the week. Then when it's time for lunch each day you can just grab one of the containers and heat it up. Things like that are going to free up more of your time then wasting more time on reading books about how to be more productive or attending seminars when in reality they should actually be getting things done.

Next you need to have a strict routine to follow. Set rules for yourself to follow each day. Things like having a wake-up time and also a sleep time. Not having enough sleep can do a lot of damage to your productivity. Funnily enough that's why cults and the military deprive people of sleep because it makes them more easy to be brainwashed. To be at your most productive, make sure that you get at least eight hours every single night.

This is so underrated but it is one of the most important things you can do. For the average person usually you need around seven and a half to eight hours of sleep. Nothing less and not more otherwise you feel tired or drowsy.

Equally important is the quality of sleep your getting and that requires the right environment. Too much light right before bed or during sleep will degrade the quality of your sleep. To many of us are staying up checking our phone before bed time. It lights up our faces and makes you anxious, especially if you get some disturbing notification. Most devices emit blue artificial lights. There are blue light blocking glasses you can wear to help or you can spend the last hours before going to sleep in a darkened room with less screen light.

A really powerful habit is to meditate before sleep in a completely darkened room. This will literally flush out all the stress of the day whilst adjusting your body to the darkness. For the best sleep results you need to be in a dark and quiet room. No phone. Get some really good sun blockers in front of your windows or at the very least use a sleeping mask. In addition, you don't want to have a lot of noise distractions. Your sleeping room should be as silent as possible. Waking up during a sleep cycle is going to have a negative affect on you the next day. Also avoid eating too much before you go to sleep. That sleep habit should be consistent from Monday to

Sunday. Keep the bedtime and wake up time consistent so that you know when your days are starting and ending. Then you can plan what you're going to do with all the hours in between.

When you really want to get things done, turn off everything and isolate yourself from distractions. You don't need to be connected to people at all times. Delete the apps that you don't need. You can always download them again later on. Things like social media are the worst offenders for distractions. Get rid of all social media whilst your working or limit your time on it. Otherwise you will be constantly in reaction. Protect your time and make sure that you're following nobody's guidance other than your own.

Social media is the biggest distraction right now. But not only that it makes people less motivated and more lazy. You see we look at the highest society lifestyle on Instagram. The girl with the hot body or the guy with the Porsche and all the money. But we don't see the hard work that went into that. Those are just snapshots of moments in time. Usually the best moments. Nobody talks about about the athlete that had to train basically his entire life in order to win the gold medal. They just talk about the nine second sprint or the celebration of the gold. Things like this are training us to ignore the hard work, heart and dedication that comes with achievements.

Your mind is like soil, the seeds you place into it grow. But if you're not taking care of that garden and removing any weeds there then the garden of your mind will be overrun with weeds that stop growth. Something powerful that you can do right now is to take one hour out of your day and write down what the main thing for you to achieve that day is. When you have written that down you need to reflect on everything you're doing in life and business that doesn't contribute to achieving whatever that main thing is. In fact this needs to be done at least every month. Even better if its every week. Take the time to review what your doing and everything that's going on in your business. Decide what needs to be done and identify the things that are holding you back.

Nowadays we are more bored than ever. It's a paradox because in reality we have the entire knowledge of humankind at our disposal on our phones. That's incredible but instead we waste our time looking at memes. Entertainment is more readily available than ever and it is everywhere. We are being over stimulated. Entertainment is all there and instant gratification is all there. However you need to avoid most of it. Now that doesn't mean throwing your phone or TV away. Instead its about being more aware of what you're feeding your mind with. As humans it's in our DNA to be stimulated by learning. But we are wasting our potentials being saturated by entertainment and instant gratification. Avoid the mainstream news and their click bait titles. Instead of mindlessly scrolling through social media or TV channels go grab a book or watch an educational YouTube channel. Learn something new and stimulate your brain.

In life and business your main priority is survival closely followed by winning. A lot of people are optimists who just try to win but in doing so many fail to see the downsides. Fact is they just look at the upside of things and think if I go to these events, read more books or start more businesses then that's more potential upside. A crucial thing is to look at both the upside and the downside of every action. In fact you should really pay more attention to the downside than the upside.

To elaborate on this point let's take a look at someone who has a goal to be fit and healthy. To achieve that goal it's fairly simple, sleep eight hours a night, exercise everyday and eat healthy food. However all this becomes incredibly complicated with all of these diet plans, training equipment, supplements, and all theses apps. The simplicity of the goal suddenly becomes very complex. Then you end up with these people with all the right shoes, apps and so on but then they eat junk food, drink alcohol and don't get enough sleep. In reality they're focusing on things with very little upside whilst ignoring the things with massive downsides.

In the business sense that could for example be working really hard but then going out every weekend and getting drunk. When it comes to Monday morning you still haven't recovered and your productivity probably doesn't return to its fullest until mid week. Then its almost Friday again and that's the night to go out drinking again. The simple action to stop drinking and going out and getting drunk would have a massive upside on your business. If you're somebody that gets drunk or high all the time and when you stop that then you'll get a huge upside. If you always eat lots of junk food then you'll have a big upside when you stop doing it. If your sleeping is always all over the place and you fix that then you will have a massive upside. If your addicted to social media and if you break that addiction then you'll have a huge upside. Think about all the consequences of all those potentially negative things in your life and the impact they have. Often things that feel good in the moment have negative second and third order consequences. Whilst many things such as exercising might feel hard in the moment but have positive second and third order consequences.

Simple things like removing sugar or sleeping properly and exercising frequently can have huge upsides. You don't need to be a gym rat, three times a week is fine. Or going for a run ten minutes a day. The thing with exercise is that it's a second order consequence where you feel the benefit. Opposite of instant gratification you get the desired result (more energy) later on. But in the moment it can be a hard task to get going with. If it helps make it fun with some group activities such as classes or team sports. Anything to get you fit and healthy. Once you get your momentum going your going to be less likely to lay in bed checking your phone. Hire either a nutrition coach or a fitness coach to then guide you and make sure you're exercising every day. Eat clean foods and cut out processed foods.

When you drink alcohol and your sleeps all over the place and if or you're not exercising and eating bad food then your emotions are going to be all over the place. Your emotions will be unpredictable, maybe in the middle of the day for no apparent reason you might start feeling worried or anxious for no real reason. When this starts happening to you then you really are screwed because your emotions have become a big turbulent pool. This makes it very hard to get things done or to make rational decisions, grow a business or do anything meaningful.

Stop being lazy

Laziness is inherent in all of us and it keeps us from living up to our potential. Without fixing it, it could potentially ruin your life. Now the craziest part is that modern life is full of traps to make us even more lazy. However there are effective long-term strategies, plus physical and mental hacks that you can use to to break free of laziness. First of all understand that laziness is both a mental and a physical issue. Which means that if you deal with both issues you will be able to kill laziness once and for all. Now as stated before the problem is that our daily life is structured to keep us lazy. Society keeps us safe, makes food readily and allows us to live a relatively comfortable life. Yes this is great but it also makes it easier than ever for us to be lazy because there is no real incentive for us to not be lazy. We have no pressure on us to step up. We stay average.

So how do you escape this and live to your fullest potential? Be mindful otherwise you fall into a bottomless pit because nobody is there to say hey change your lifestyle. Or nobody is there to say hey maybe go work and hustle hard if you want to reach your dreams. The only person there is you and you have to be in control of your life and bring awareness into it so that you avoid these daily life traps. Instant gratification is the biggest culprit of making you lazy.

On a physical issue right away, there are things you can avoid. First of all avoid processed food. It tastes good when you eat it in the moment. You get that instant gratification but then all of a sudden you feel really tired. On top of that if your tired go and drink coffee and then you'll be fine. Take this pill and you will instantly be more focused. But it's all a quick fix and combined into a vicious circle. Take the magic pill no need to worry about changing your habits and lifestyle. Go ahead and eat pizza and if you are feeling tired, go drink a coffee. Then if your dehydrated have a sugary can of soda which will make you crash and spike again.

Round and round goes the vicious cycle of laziness. Well imagine eating this for years at a time. That doesn't mean you need to cut it out forever. Eating junk food every now and then is totally fine but overall in general you want to eat clean. That will give you more energy and less likelihood to be lazy. The crazy thing is you can actually become addicted to sitting on your couch watching TV and eating junk food. I'm sure you know exactly what im talking about, we have all been there. But the other crazy thing is that you can also addict yourself to going to the gym, living a healthy lifestyle and eating clean. Your body will become addicted to something no matter what. Therefore you might as well make it addicted to something positive which makes you less lazy.

Now we have covered the physical side of overcoming laziness, let's take a look at the mental aspect of getting over laziness. Earlier on I mentioned that learning new things is beneficial. You need to be in control of your mind and not have some external sources or entertainment controlling you. Another way to stimulate your mind is meditation. This is one of the best ways to train you in controlling your mind. Ask most successful people whether they meditate or not and I'm sure most of them will tell you that they do. Now you don't have to be religious or spiritual. Meditation is very simple, it's simply about letting go of thoughts and clearing your mind. In doing so your letting go of addiction to distraction and allowing yourself to live in the present moment. Learning meditation is really easy these days and there's tons of videos about it which you could just find on YouTube.

Another thing that most successful people have which helps them be more productive and of course less lazy is to have a higher purpose and a dream to live. Earlier on we set some goals and by constantly being aware of them this will drive your life forward. they should be strong enough goals for you to be compelled to not be lazy. But if that's not enough then you can add in a morning routine. Without structure in your day you will be likely to dabble. Maybe you go get some coffee, check facebook or stare out the window. That dabbling can be fixed by having a structure throughout the day which begins with a morning routine. That could be waking up, writing down your goals, meditation then planning the day. On a broader scale you can create a structure throughout the week, month and for years ahead.

The mornings are the times where we tend to dabble the most. But it is also the time when are brain is at its freshest. Everybody can create their own custom morning routine depending on their goals. For example if your goals are health and fitness it could be about getting and up you going to the bathroom you weigh yourself first thing. Then you drink some water, have a healthy breakfast and then workout.

Essentially with a morning routine you want to be able to know what you have to do step by step so that you set yourself up for success and avoid the traps. Ideally you don't check your emails or notifications because that puts you on somebody else's time schedule. The mornings should be a sacred time which you protect to do things that give you energy for the day ahead. Spend some time to read, meditate or experiment around with getting certain morning routines in but it's important that you have a routine. Check out my other book for more on this.

[Morning Routine: Skyrocket Your Productivity, Enhance Your Energy & Achieve Your Goals With A Fully Optimized Morning Ritual](#)

We are now living in a society where being lazy is accepted. Take a stand against it, cut out the processed foods and instead eat clean. Cut out negative mind stimulations and anything that is instantly gratifying. Introduce awareness to what you fill your mind with. Control the stimulus that comes into your mind. Exercise and get your best high quality sleep in. Find your purpose and let it guide you.

Conclusion

Living your dream life is something that so many of us strive to do. But too many people live their whole lives without ever really discovering who they are. They never challenge themselves. Time passes by and they remain the same but somewhat safe in their own comfort zones. Life is always pushing against us and if you don't push back harder it will push you further back.

Discovering yourself and living your dream life is not going to happen if your always surrounded by the same familiar things and the same people everyday. It's not going to happen to you. Escape your comfort zone, be clear about your goals and then take a leap of faith into the unknown. Taking a leap of faith is a step towards self discovery. Breaking out of your routine life will present you with new experiences, challenges and people that will reveal things about yourself that you never knew.

Life can be unpredictable for the most part. For the majority of us we are living in fear of the unknown and so we stay with what we know. Because outside of our familiar surroundings are the things that we cannot predict and the things that might make us uncomfortable. But if you dare to take a leap into the unknown then it could be life changing for you. Life should be one big adventure.

Now if the thought of all this overwhelms or scares you, then reframe it as a sign to be excited. Reflect back on your life. When was the last time you took a leap of faith or took a risk? Maybe it was so long ago you can barely remember the feeling. But I'm sure there is something in your past to reflect on. Take some time to reflect on that experience. How did it go? What was the result? I'm sure you were afraid at first but in the end you gained a lot of benefits. Even if it was a failure, I'm sure it taught you some valuable life lessons. You see the more you try new things, take risks and leaps of faith the less fear you will have because our fears start disappear when we face them. Ultimately the person who consistently throws themselves into the unknown and unpredictable situations gains more confidence and inner strength.

Think about what you would like to change in your life. What do you need to do to make that happen? Follow your intuition because it's the true essence of your feelings and instincts about what you really want in your life. For most of us we ignore these because the thought of them is so scary. I can testify to this. A number of years ago I always had the dream of traveling overseas for an extended period of time. But I was comfortable in a stable job. I was safe and I could have ignored that dream. I did that for a while but the feeling would not go away. I followed that feeling and one day I resigned but two days later I took back the decision because of fear. I was afraid of things not working out, of not having enough money, of being too old. Afraid of coming back with nothing. Every excuse, I had. For the next few months I debated against myself all the time until finally I really did resign. Only this time my boss told me there would be no coming back. The bridges were burned and at the end of the month I boarded a plane to a new life. At that time all I had was $600 in my bank account. That was eight years ago and now I'm still traveling, grateful for that decision because it changed my life for the better. It allowed me to work in the areas I am passionate about and to be where I want to be.

A leap of faith can never really be guaranteed to be successful or not. But it's better than doing nothing. It might lead to something better. In my example where I quit my job to travel this is a case in point. That job which I took initially was supposed to be my leap of faith. I had recently broken up with my long term girlfriend. So I saw this new job in the big city and took it. However it wasn't what I wanted but the journey took me towards my real dreams. Because as we discussed leaps of faith are ways forward to self discovery and a better life. Ultimately, if you feel that there is more to life and you really want to change your life then your going to have to take a leap of faith. Do or do not, there is no try.

I would like to relate this to a film. Have you ever seen the film Indiana Jones and the Last Crusade? Whilst searching for Holy Grail Indiana Jones comes across a broken pathway on a cliff edge. On the other side is a doorway to the Holy Grail. But there is no bridge to cross the abyss. However in the map there is a picture of a man stepping across. He seems to be walking across an invisible bridge. Indiana Jones needs to take that leap of faith to cross the abyss. He steps out and in doing so finds that there is an invisible bridge to walk across. To find your Holy Grail you too must have the strength to take that leap of faith.

Remove your excuses. Believe me I probably had better ones. We are only on planet earth for a limited time, so why waste it? Don't let society make the decision for you. When you take responsibility for your life and live on your terms then great things and opportunities will start to happen. People will come into your life. This is because you have made the space for them and have set the intent from your heart. But that can only happen when you throw yourself into the unknown and surrender to your heart and soul. If you believe in your dreams then you can have them. First you need to have faith in yourself.

Living the life of your dreams will certainly mean making big changes in your life. That could be in your career, location or relationships. Think about your life and what you want and what you don't want. What are the things or people that hold you back? Maybe you live in a small boring town. Or maybe your relationship has been holding you back for the last few years. Or maybe you want to reinvent yourself. All of that is fine but you need to be clear on whether you really want that or not.

Keep on coming up with new ideas and cultivate a strong mindset to navigate through the oceans of success. Sometimes you will have setbacks but if you have a success mindset then you can always bounce back. Ask any rich person if they lost everything could they make it all back? Most will tell you yes and they really believe that they can. Donald Trump was once billions of dollars in debt. He turned it around and became president of The United States. Anthony Joshua was beaten by an underdog in New York and embarrassed in front of the world. He lost all his boxing belts but he turned it around and won them back six months later. Turn your life around.

Being true to yourself about what you want and moving towards are the first steps to living your dream life. By understanding and knowing yourself is about more than preferences it's about who you are true core of your soul. Self discovery is never too late and going after your goals can happen at any age. You too can still take that leap of faith.

Each day we are presented with various new ways to become stronger and break that comfort zone. We need to build that muscle to break free and seek joy in the discomfort. That could be as simple cold showers in the morning or talking to strangers. The most important thing is to be aware that the best things in life usually come from breaking through our comfort zones. The more you push yourself to take on small challenges the easier it will be to face the bigger ones. Treat each day as an adventure that will test you. Every day of your life you are making a choice to either stay in your comfort zone or live your life to the fullest. It's always up to you, you are in control.

It's time to open a new chapter in your life.

Resources

Carnegie, Dale. How to Win Friends and Influence People. Vermilion; New Ed edition (6 April 2006).

Colleges Admissions Service (UCAS) (1992 founded). UK.

Ferrazi, Keith. Never Eat Alone (2014). Penguin.

Ferris, Tim. (2007). The 4-hour Workweek. Vermilion.

Kiyosaki, Robert (1997). Rich Dad Poor Dad. Plata Publishing.

Kiyosaki, Robert (2014). Robert Kiyosaki quote.

Lucas, George. Spielberg, Steven. (1989). Indiana Jones and The Last Crusade. Lucasfim Ltd.

National Center for Education Statistics (1867 founded). Washington, D.C., United States.

Montfort, Oscar. (2019). Morning Routine: Skyrocket Your Productivity, Enhance Your Energy & Achieve Your Goals With A Fully Optimized Morning Ritual. Fortune Publishing.

Ovens, Sam (2018-2019). Sam Ovens Consulting.

Peterson, Jordan (2018). Jordan Peterson Twitter account.

Small Business Administration. https://www.sba.gov/

Twain, Mark. (1835-1910). Mark Twain quote.

Rituals Of The Rich & Famous

Success Tips, Strategies and Habits of The Rich & Famous

Get 4 new strategies every week on how to be more productive, confident, and happy.

Get Access Now

www.ingramcontent.com/pod-product-compliance
Lightning Source LLC
Chambersburg PA
CBHW070118110526
44587CB00014BA/2199